the Glory of Revelation

An In-Depth Study Guide on the Book of Revelation

ANNE GRANT

WestBow
PRESS
A DIVISION OF THOMAS NELSON

Quotations marked "NLT" are from the Holy Bible, New Living Translation. Copyright 1996, 2004, Wheaton, Illinois: Tyndale Publishers, Inc.

Quotations marked "KJV" are from the King James Version of the Bible. Copyright 1997, Wheaton, Illinois: Tyndale Publishers, Inc.

All other quotations are from the New International Version of the Bible. Copyright 1984, Grand Rapids, Michigan. Used by permission of Zondervan.

WestBow Press books may be ordered through booksellers or by contacting:

WestBow Press
A Division of Thomas Nelson
1663 Liberty Drive
Bloomington, IN 47403
www.westbowpress.com
1-(866) 928-1240

ISBN: 978-1-4497-4795-4 (sc)
ISBN: 978-1-4497-4794-7 (hc)
ISBN: 978-1-4497-4796-1 (e)

Library of Congress Control Number: 2012906488

Printed in the United States of America

WestBow Press rev. date: 04/24/2012

I thank my loving husband, Tony, whose prayers encouraged me to never give up; and my son, Tony Jr., and my daughters, Odetta and Sherise, for their patience and loving support. I would also like to thank Bethsheva Lightbourne, Samantha Ferguson, and Tasman Sutherland for their assistance.

Contents

Preface   ix

About the Author   xi

Introduction   1

Chapter 1:   This Coming Glory   7

Chapter 2:   The Power and Glory of Worship   20

Chapter 3:   Message to the Seven Churches   32

Chapter 4:   The Rapture of the Church   54

Chapter 5:   When That Trumpet Sounds   60

Chapter 6:   Glimpses into Christ's Glory   63

Chapter 7:   A Greater Unfolding of God's Power and Glory   78

Chapter 8:   The Cosmic Conflict between God and
             Satan: Part One   86

Chapter 9:   The Cosmic Conflict between God and
             Satan: Part Two   100

Chapter 10: The Antichrist   116

Chapter 11: A Further Glimpse into Eternity   122

Chapter 12: The Seven Bowls of the Seven Plagues   128

Chapter 13: The Great Prostitute   137

Chapter 14: Rapid Glory!   141

Chapter 15: Thousand-Year Millennium Reign   154

Chapter 16: A New Age   162

Conclusion: Life Forever in the Glory   175

Preface

In 1998, after an unusually long illness, as I sat in the presence of the Lord asking for more of His glorious fragrance, the Holy Spirit spoke to me. He spoke as the Spirit of wisdom. He told me that if I wanted more, then I should study the life and the sayings of Jesus Christ. I was to read the four gospels and books of Acts and Revelation at least once a year.

He told me to begin with Revelation, then read the four gospels, and end with the book of Acts. Today I am reaping the benefit of obedience. This continued act of obedience has opened and is continually increasing my understanding of the richness of the Christian faith. It has also revealed to me the deep love of God for His church—the bride of Christ.

This exercise has made me a more committed believer and has heightened my awareness of God. It has disclosed to me the awesome truth of His abiding presence in my life during the good and bad times. My faith journey has been empowered, and my love for God's Word has increased. The book of Revelation has given me a deeper appreciation for the finished work of Jesus Christ. The writing of John unveils the full identity of Christ. It reveals His majestic power and glory that are eternal. He will reign forever and ever.

As you read this book, may you go beyond the timetable of events and John's symbolic style of literature to the great truth of the author's revelation of Jesus. During my studies, I was remembering the prophets of old, their great prophecies concerning God's glory, and how it all correlates with John's revelation. In Habakkuk 2:14, the prophet proclaimed, "For the time will come when all the earth will be filled, as the waters fill the sea, with an awareness of the glory of the Lord." Again in Isaiah 11:9b, we hear the prophetic utterance coming forth. "And as the waters fill the sea, so the earth will be filled with people who know the Lord."

I also remembered Daniel's earlier vision of Jesus Christ. "As my vision continued that night, I saw someone like a son of man coming with the clouds of heaven. He approached the Ancient One and was led into His presence. He was given authority, honor, and sovereignty over all the nations of the world, so that people of every race and nation and language would obey Him. His rule is eternal—it will never end. His kingdom will never be destroyed" (Daniel 7:13-14 NLT). Truly this is what John's revelation is all about. Jesus is the amen and the glory! This book reveals to you God's plan for this earth to once again be filled with His glory. It is a book on God's ever-increasing glory.

About the Author

Pastor Anne Grant was born in Ragged Island, Bahamas. She is an international anointed prophetess, evangelist, and conference speaker with a dynamic personal touch in ministry. Her gentle spirit communicates the deep truths of God's Word as she confidently shares. Called by God for this time, her life-changing teaching will bring freedom and joy to your life. Pastor Anne has experienced what it means to go through the fire and through the flood.

Pastor Anne is also the author of *The Fragrance of Glory* and *The Power of Prayer and Fasting*. She studied at Atlantic Baptist College in New Brunswick, Canada, and Jacksonville Theological Seminary in Jacksonville, Florida. She holds a bachelor's degree in Christian psychology and a master's degree in theology. Anne and her husband, Tony, are the founders and pastors of A Call to Holiness Ministries, Agape House in Freeport, Bahamas.

Pastors Tony and Anne have been married for over forty years and are the parents of three grown children.

The Glory of Revelation

Meaning of Revelation—Act of knowing . . . revealing. It is a translation of the Greek word *apocalyptic* (a-pok-a-ly-sis), which means uncovering of something that is concealed. **"The time is coming when everything that is covered up will be revealed, and all that is secret will be made known to all"** (Luke 12:2 NLT). We are now living in that time. There is great exposure taking place in the body of Christ that will continue to increase as the glory increases. Sin will be exposed at every level as God purifies His church for Christ's return. **"For the time has come for judgment, and it must begin with God's household"** (1 Peter 4:17 NLT).

Introduction

Revelation is a revealing of Jesus Christ given by Himself to John His servant for the benefit of His church. It reveals the face and the hand of Jesus the great trustee of divine revelation. He alone holds the key to everything that has been sealed. He has been given absolute authority over the church. **"Now He is far above any ruler or authority or power or leader or anything else—not only in this world but also in the world to come. God has put all things under the authority of Christ and has made Him head over all things for the benefit of the Church"** (Ephesians 1:21-22 NLT). God gave this revelation to Jesus Christ to show us His servants what must soon take place. Jesus sent an angel to present this revelation to John on the isle of Patmos. John faithfully reported everything He saw and was given. **"This is a revelation from Jesus Christ, which God gave him to show His servants what must soon take place. He sent an angel to present this revelation to His servant John, who faithfully reported everything he saw. This is his report of the word of God and the testimony of Jesus Christ"** (Revelation 1:1-2 NLT).

Revelation reveals Jesus' evaluation of His church sixty to sixty-five years after His ascension. Through His letters to the churches, Jesus graded the churches' spiritual well-being. He examined their spiritual heart life, the way they loved and pointed out the good and the bad. His assessment of the churches was to strengthen his servants and to encourage faithfulness and truth as they follow the Master's plan. In Jesus, every situation in a believer's life is a win-win. **"The thief's**

purpose is to steal and kill and destroy. My purpose is to give them a rich and satisfying life" (John 10:10 NLT).

Authorship: The apostle John (John the Revelator), whose name means "The Lord is gracious," was also known as the "beloved apostle." "The disciple Jesus loved was sitting next to Jesus at the table" (John 13:23 NLT). He occupied the place next to Jesus at the Last Supper. It is believed that John was the only one of Jesus' twelve disciples who was not killed for the faith.

John wrote the fourth gospel (the book of John), the three Johannine Epistles (1, 2, and 3 John) and the book of Revelation. The writings for this book were given to John in a vision while he was in exile on the island of Patmos. Most scholars believe that the actual writing took place after John had left the island of his exile, but the vision was given to him while on the island.

He was in exile because of His testimony of Jesus Christ. "I, John, am your brother and your partner in suffering and in God's kingdom and in the patient endurance to which Jesus calls us. I was exiled to the island of Patmos for preaching the word of God and for my testimony about Jesus" (Revelation 1:9 NLT). Tradition has it that John lived to an extreme old age, dying at Ephesus. The true servant of God never retires on the earth. Our retirement package is in heaven to be enjoyed at the completion of the race. Retirement was never an option for Abraham. He received his promise well after the age of retirement. Moses received his call as God's leader at the age of eighty, and all the mighty men and women of God completed their course despite their age. God will use a faithful believer of any age to show His glory on the earth.

The vision John saw was indescribable, so he used symbols and illustrations to show what it was like. As a reader, you will never understand every minute detail of this great book, nor should you try to. Let your focus be on the gist of the vision, which tells us that Jesus Christ is the glory of God, the Lamb, the Lion of the tribe of Judah, and the conquering

King of Kings and Lord of Lords who will come again in the fullness of His splendor and glory to reign forever and ever!

God used John's exile to unfold the return of Christ and His great victory over evil. Christ will reign victorious as King of Kings and Lord of Lords forever! God will always use a faithful Christian's suffering to unfold more of His glory on the earth. Because you are faithful, whatever you go through is always for God's glory. He will produce from your pain and shame another story for his glory. When the Devil thinks that he has won, God's power and glory have just begun!

The book of Revelation shows us Christ in all His power and glory.

- Chapter One—He is revealed as the glorious, victorious, all-powerful King who rules forever and ever.

- Chapter Two—The One who walks among the golden lampstands and has authority over the church and its leader.

- Chapter Three—The One who is holy and true. He holds the key of David. He opens doors no one can shut.

- Chapter Four—The Creator and Sustainer of everything, both great and small.

- Chapter Five—The Lion but yet the Lamb. He is the Lion of the tribe of Judah, the heir to David's throne, and the Lamb that was slain for the sins of the world.

- Chapters Six, Seven, Eight, and Nine—The Perfect Lamb that was worthy to take the scroll and break its seals and open it.

- Chapters Ten and Eleven—One who lives and reigns forever and ever. The One who created the heavens, earth, seas, and everything in them. The whole world has now become the kingdom of our Lord and of His Christ.

- Chapters Twelve, Thirteen, Fourteen, and Fifteen—His ultimate triumph over evil. He is the conquering Lamb of glory who sits as Judge.

- Chapters Sixteen, Seventeen, and Eighteen—The Defender of our faith whose punishments are true and just.

- Chapter Nineteen—He is the faithful and true Word of God, the Commander of heaven's armies.

- Chapter Twenty—He will reign as Commander-in-Chief in the life of His church forever.

- Chapters Twenty-One and Twenty-Two—He is the light of that everlasting city, the Alpha and Omega—the beginning and the end—the Keeper of the Lamb's Book of Life, the Bright and Morning Star, the Faithful Witness, the Source of David, the Heir to his throne, and the amen.

You are worthy, O Lord our God,

To receive glory and honor and power.

For you created everything,

and it is for your pleasure that they exist and were created.

Revelation 4:11 NLT

QUESTIONS FOR REVIEW

1. How many books of the Bible were written by John the Revelator?

2. Name the books of the Bible that were written by John.

3. How many of Jesus' disciples are believed to have been killed for their faith?

4. Why was John on the isle of Patmos?

5. What is meant by the phrase, "I John was worshipping in the Spirit"?

6. What is the gist of John's vision?

7. According to the book of Revelation, who is Jesus Christ?

8. What is the meaning of John's name?

9. As a believer, you encounter occasional persecution and pain. How do they affect your worship?

CHAPTER ONE

This Coming Glory

Revelation 1:1-8

Revelation is the only book in the Bible that promises a blessing to those who listen to its words and do what it says. **"God blesses the one who reads the words of this prophecy to the Church, and He blesses all who listen to the message and obey what it says, for the time is near"** (Revelation 1:3 NLT). As believers, we are called upon to listen to the message and obey what it says. This conveys the importance of this book, which concerns not only end-time prophecy but also instructs and shares great truths that will not only make us knowledgeable, wise, and happy but will also keep us experiencing the high favor of God as we obey.

This book lists six other blessings promised to believers:

1) **"And I heard a voice from heaven saying, 'Write this down: Blessed are those who die in the Lord from now on. Yes, says the Spirit, they are blessed indeed, for they will rest from their hard work; for their good deeds follow them!'"** (Revelation 14:13 NLT). What a blessing to know that our "good deeds" will follow us out of time and into eternity! Only what is done for Christ will last. Everything else, including our money, fortune, and fame, cannot be taken beyond the grave.

But the good deeds of men that bring honor and glory to God will follow us and provide an immeasurable reward.

2. **"Look, I will come as unexpectedly as a thief! Blessed are all who are watching for me, who keep their clothing ready so they will not have to walk around naked and ashamed"** (Revelation 16:15 NLT). As believers, we must be watching for the unexpected return of Christ. We don't want to be like the five foolish virgins in the parable of the ten. They were not ready for the Bridegroom's return. We want to be ready for His glorious appearance.

3. **"And the angel said to me, 'Write this: Blessed are those who are invited to the wedding feast of the Lamb.' And he added, 'These are true words that come from God'"** (Revelation 19:9 NLT). What a high privilege to be invited to the wedding feast of the Lamb! In the parable of the great feast, Jesus tells the story of how the invitees all made excuses and turned down the invitation. As believers, may we be careful not to excuse ourselves from this invitation by becoming too busy with our own concerns and placing the Lord's on hold.

4. **"Blessed and holy are those who share in the first resurrection, for them the second death holds no power, but they will be priests of God and of Christ and will reign with Him a thousand years"** (Revelation 20:6 NLT). The reign of Christ in the hearts of believers exempts them from the power of the second death. During the millennium, the believers (priests of God) will be reigning with Jesus.

5. **"Look, I am coming soon! Blessed are those who obey the words of prophecy written in this book"** (Revelation 22:7 NLT). Jesus again points to His "soon" return. It is true that no man knows the day or the hour, but we should live in an attitude of expectation. We are admonished to obey the words that have been given to us in this book.

6. **"Blessed are those who wash their robes. They will be permitted to enter through the gates of the city and eat the fruit from the Tree of Life"** (Revelation 22:14 NLT). As believers, we must keep our hearts pure. It is only the pure in heart who will be able to enter the gates of the New Jerusalem and partake from the Tree of Life.

Revelation was written to the seven churches in the province of Asia. The number *seven* is used throughout Scripture to symbolize completeness, fullness, and perfection. This truth was introduced to us in Genesis, the book of beginnings. **"On the seventh day, having finished His task, God rested from all His work. And God blessed the seventh day and declared it holy because it was the day when He rested from all His work of creation"** (Genesis 2:2-3 NLT). In the book of Revelation, the number seven seems to represent all churches throughout the church age *(Life in the Spirit Study Bible Commentary)*.[1] We are still in the church age, and the spiritual condition of the churches today is very much like the seven churches in the province of Asia to whom these letters were written. All of them (except for one) were given commendation, and five of them were given rebukes because of their major spiritual problems.

Sevenfold Spirit—"This letter is from John to the Seven Churches in the province of Asia. Grace and peace to you from the One who is, who always was, and who is still to come; from the Sevenfold Spirit before His throne; and from Jesus Christ" (Revelation 1:4-5a). In John's letters to the seven churches, he brought them greetings of grace and peace from the triune God: Father, Son, and Holy Spirit. He refers to the Holy Spirit as "the Sevenfold Spirit" before God's throne.

This term does not mean that there are seven spirits but rather suggests to us the ministries of the one Holy Spirit. It represents the perfection and the ministry of the Holy Spirit to the church and describes the

---

[1]   *Life in the Spirit Study Bible Commentary*, p. 2039.

sevenfold fullness of the Holy Spirit. One characteristic of this sevenfold fullness is that the Holy Spirit is *complete*. He is not a *part* of God; He is completely God. The Holy Spirit is the Spirit of God; all that God is and forevermore will be has been given to us as our Enabler. **"Not by might, nor by power, but by my Spirit, says the Lord of Almighty"** (Zechariah 4:6b NIV). **"But I will send you the Counselor—the Spirit of truth. He will come to you from the Father and will tell you all about me"** (John 15:26 NLT).

The Holy Spirit is God's power force on the earth today. He is the Spirit of truth and glory. All holiness, righteousness, truth, wisdom, knowledge, and understanding flow through Him into the lives of ready believers. He is the *Holy* Spirit, the very essence of holiness. He is the fulfilled promise of Jesus to His church. He is the Spirit of the Lord, the Spirit of grace and glory dwelling in the lives of believers.

The ministry of the Sevenfold Spirit in the life of the church: **"'The future glory of this temple will be greater than the past glory,' says the Lord of heaven's armies"** (Haggai 2:9a NLT). If we are going to experience the latter fullness of God's glory, if we are going to complete our mandate and not give in to the plans of the Devil to weaken us and cause us to fail, and if we are going to continually move at God's speed, then the sevenfold fullness (ministries) of the Spirit of Glory—the Holy Spirit—must be known and operational in the church. The sevenfold ministries of the Holy Spirit may also be known as *God's management team* that has been sent to the body of Christ—His church—to complete the glorious work of the kingdom.

As God's management team on earth, the sevenfold anointing of the Holy Spirit makes the glory of God visible on the earth. God's management team enables us to live a life in the Spirit while we are living in these earthly bodies. The power and anointing of the Holy Spirit will transform us into overcomers. There are times when the Lord will allow us to go through some trials, difficulties, and disappointments to strengthen our spiritual wings of faith so that we are prepared to overcome the next storm in our lives. The Holy Spirit will always be our

Alongsider along life's way. **"But when the Father sends the Advocate as my representative—that is the Holy Spirit—He will teach you everything and will remind you of everything I have told you"** (John 14:26 NLT).

To perceive a clearer picture of God's management team, we must take a look at Isaiah 11:1-2. **"Out of the stump of David's family will grow a shoot—yes, a new Branch bearing fruit from the old root. And the Spirit of the Lord will rest on Him, the Spirit of wisdom and understanding, the Spirit of counsel and might, the Spirit of knowledge and the fear of the Lord."** Jesus was that shoot, the new branch that came bearing fruit from the old root. He walked in this power and anointing during His earthly ministry, and He was able to overcome the Devil at every level.

Before He returned to glory, He delegated this power to His church, enabling us to overcome the Devil at every level. **"I have been given all authority in heaven and on earth. Therefore go and make disciples of all nations, baptizing them in the name of the Father and the Son and the Holy Spirit"** (Matthew 28:18 NLT). This delegated power is only made visible when the believer's life is control by the presence of the God Spirit—the Holy Spirit. When our lives are being governed by His Spirit, we operate on the earth under the authority of heaven. His management team, the sevenfold fullness of the Holy Spirit, will be made visible in the church.

The power of Christ is displayed in His church through the sevenfold fullness of the Holy Spirit. As the church is prepared for this final great end-time revival, we will begin to understand and operate through the incredible greatness of this power that is available to all believers.

Let's take a look at the sevenfold fullness of the Holy Spirit (God's management team for believers).

The Sevenfold Spirit before the Throne

"From the sevenfold Spirit before His throne . . ."

In the fourth verse, it does not say sevenfold *spirits*, but sevenfold *spirit*, suggesting that it is the one Spirit demonstrating the fullness of God among men. Out of the one Spirit flow the spirits of wisdom, understanding, counsel, might, knowledge, and the fear of the Lord. John saw all of who God was and is and evermore shall be; he saw the fullness, power, and the splendor of His glory. He saw the sevenfold anointing of the Holy Spirit as it flows from the throne of God.

The Sevenfold Spirit Is God's Glory Management Team

God does nothing without His management team—the sevenfold spirit. When Jesus said, **"Lo, I come (in the volume of the book it is written of me,) to do thy will, O God"** (Hebrews 10:7 KJV). Jesus said this, indicating that He came as all God. He came as the power and glory of God. He came as the wisdom of God, as the understanding of God, as the counsel of God, the might of God, as the knowledge of God and the fear of the Lord.

What an awesome thought! God sent all that He was, is, and evermore shall be, to be poured out as a drink offering for the sins of man—what love! Before Jesus went away, His promise was that this same Holy Spirit would govern the church until He returned. **"But I will send you the Advocate—the Spirit of truth. He will come to you from the Father and will testify all about me"** (John 15:26 NLT). This sevenfold fullness of the Holy Spirit, the Spirit of glory (God's glory management team), manages the life of the church. This fullness will take us beyond earth's limitations into the glory of God and keep us there.

A More In-Depth Look at God's Management Team

- **The Spirit of the Lord is both the anointing and the source of the anointing.** He creates the very life of God within us. It is through the Spirit of God that we are able to crucify the old self. **"My old self has been crucified with Christ. It is no longer I who live, but Christ lives in me. So I live in this earthly body by trusting in the Son of God"** (Galatians 2:20 NLT).

- **The Spirit of wisdom is the supernatural intelligence of God.** Oh how the church needs to be flowing in the wisdom, the supernatural intelligence of God! The Spirit of wisdom is the essence of all God's thoughts. **"By wisdom the Lord laid the earth's foundation"** (Proverbs 3:19a NLT). The wisdom of the world will kill you. The wisdom of God will save you. It will add years to your life by helping you to make the right choices. James told the church, **"If you need wisdom—if you want to know what God wants you to do—ask Him, and He will gladly tell you. He will not resent your asking"** (James 1-5 NLT). Paul told the church in Corinth that Jesus is both the power and wisdom of God to all those called by God to salvation. **"This foolish plan of God is wiser than the wisest of human plans, and God's weakness is stronger than the greatest of human strength"** (1 Corinthians 1:25 NLT).

  o King Solomon recognized this need for godly wisdom. When he came to the throne, he did not ask for worldly riches. He requested godly wisdom to lead God's people. **"Give me the wisdom and knowledge to lead them properly, or who could possibly govern this great people of yours?"** (2 Chronicles 1:10 NLT). Oh, how we need the prayer of Solomon among our leaders today, that the power **and the glory of God may be displayed in our services.**

- **The Spirit of understanding works hand in hand with wisdom.** The Spirit of understanding entails God's illuminations and insights released through the revelation of His Holy Word. **"By understanding he set the heavens in place"** (Proverbs 3:19b NLT). Understanding brings life to our souls and helps us to keep from falling and crippling our faith. **We acquire understanding through a right relationship with God.** We cannot relate to the ways of God or others unless we have understanding. In Luke we read, **"Then He opened their minds to understand these many Scriptures"** (Luke 24:45 NLT). The Spirit of understanding will give you the ability to interpret God's Word and apply it to your daily living.

- **The Spirit of counsel is our advocate.** As Jesus prepared to return to the Father, He knew that His church would need spiritual support at all times and in every season of its being. He told them, **"No, I will not abandon you as orphans—I will come to you"** (John 14:18 NLT). Again He said, **"And I will ask the Father, and He will give you another Advocate, who will never leave you. He is the Holy Spirit who leads into all truth . . . but when the Father sends the Advocate as my representative—that is, the Holy Spirit—he will teach you everything and will remind you of everything I have told you"** (John 14:16-17a, 26 NLT). Jesus did not leave us as orphans. We have the Spirit of counsel among us. He will lead and guide us into all truth. We can freely seek his counsel, knowing that He will not withhold it from us. We need times of refreshing from the Spirit of counsel so that our lives will show forth the glory of God!

- **The Spirit of might is God's power to do His will on the earth.** We are given God's energy and power to become all that He desires of us and to do His will. **"For God is working in you, giving you the desire and the power to do what pleases him"** (Philippians 2:13 NLT). As a believer, there should never be a season of defeat in your life. We are to go on from victory to victory because of the Spirit of might, God's power in our lives.

o   The Spirit of might helps us to put off the habits of the flesh and overcome them with its passions, thereby putting on Christ. This Spirit helps us to clothe ourselves in the mind of Christ and to fulfill the will of God for our lives. When our human strength fails, it is the Spirit of might that carries us. **"So now I am glad to boast about my weaknesses, so that the power of Christ can work through me . . . for when I am weak, then I am strong"** (2 Corinthians 12:9b; 10b NLT).

* **The Spirit of knowledge is the ability to perceive and know truth.** Your knowledge of God will keep you focused on spiritual matters. You will continually be able to overcome the world, flesh, and the Devil. **"And you will know the truth, and the truth will set you free"** (John 8:32 NLT). Knowledge is power and the more knowledge you have of God, the more powerful will be your life as a believer. No matter the test or struggle in your life, your faith will remain grounded and rooted in His word. Job's testimony during his darkest hour was one of knowing. **"But as for me, I know that my Redeemer lives and he will stand upon the earth at last. And after my body has decayed, yet in my body I will see God!"** (Job 19:25 NLT).

The Spirit of the Fear of the Lord—holy reverence and respect for the awesomeness, majesty, holiness, and glory of God. The Bible says, **"Serve the Lord with reverent fear, and rejoice with trembling"** (Psalm 2:11 NLT). The Spirit of the fear of the Lord teaches us to have reverential fear of Him. It is not suggesting your being terrified of God but honoring and recognizing His holiness and standing in awe of His majesty. It will propel us to walk in love and true holiness, thus creating a strong atmosphere for the Spirit of the Lord to move in our midst. It lengthens one's life and provides security. **"Fear of the Lord lengthens one's life, but the years of the wicked are cut short"** (Proverbs 10:27 NLT). **"Those who fear the Lord are secure; he will be a refuge for their children. Fear of the Lord is a life-giving fountain; it offers escape from the snares of death"** (Proverbs 14:26-27 NLT). It will usher in the *shekinah* glory. It is my daily prayer that as believers we will allow the Spirit of the fear of the Lord into our lives to empower us to walk in the blessings of the Lord.

We need the sevenfold fullness (anointing) of God (His management team) in operation in our lives. The world is looking for more than a good sermon. Christians want to see the demonstration of the power and the glory of the sermons that are able to move mountains and set the captive free. We need a fresh baptism into God so that His fire and glory may be revealed. We need an *upper room experience* where we can release all to God and receive all from Him.

In the upper room, the disciples tarried and waited for the promised Holy Spirit to come and filled their lives. Something phenomenal happened to those discipleswhile they waited. God made His presence known to them in an incredible way that transformed their lives forever. The church today needs to experience its own Pentecost. Our lives need to be soaked in His presence so that the glory may fall.

The book of Revelation is about the power and glory of God. It shows us Jesus Christ in all His triumphal power and glory. His second coming is indescribable! In writing to the churches, John burst out in high praise and worship of the Christ who came and freed us from our sins and is coming again to take us with Him **"All glory to Him who loves us and has freed us from our sins by shedding His blood for us. He has made us a kingdom of priests for God His Father. All glory and power to Him forever and ever! Amen. Look! He comes with the clouds of heaven. And everyone will see Him—even those who pierced Him. And all the nations of the world will mourn for him. Yes! Amen! "I am the Alpha and Omega—the beginning and the end," says the**

Lord God. "I am the one who is, who always was, and who is still to come—The Almighty One" (Revelation 1:5b-8 NLT).

As we read this book and discover the glory of His revelation to John, may we too burst forth in high praise and worship of His coming power and ever-increasing glory. May we sing like Charles Gabriel: "O that will be glory for me, glory for me, glory for me, when by His grace I shall look at His face, that will be glory, glory for me" (Charles H. Gabriel, 1900, "O That Will Be Glory").

QUESTIONS FOR REVIEW

1. How many blessings are listed in the book of Revelation? Name them.

2. What are some of the promises listed in these blessings?

3. The number seven is used in the book of Revelation as a symbol of _____ and _____.

4. What is the number seven symbolic of in Genesis 2:2?

5. How is the sevenfold Spirit of God described in Isaiah 11:2?

6. Describe the Spirit of the Lord.

7. Describe the Spirit of wisdom.

8. Describe the Spirit of counsel.

9. Describe the Spirit of might.

10. Describe the Spirit of Knowledge.

11. Describe the Spirit of the fear of the Lord.

12. Give another name for the sevenfold Spirit of God.

13. What is the primary purpose of the book of Revelation?

14. Is there more than one Spirit? How is your life being managed by God?

CHAPTER TWO

The Power and Glory of Worship

Revelation 1:9-20

The Glory of Pure Worship!

**"It was the Lord's day, and I was worshipping in the Spirit . . ."
(Revelation 1:10 NLT).** The state of John's physical condition did not
distract him from worship. He was immersed in worship on the Lord's
Day. John tells us that he was in the Spirit worshipping on the Lord's
Day. The Spirit had taken over his mental and physical strength and
pure worship flowed from his being. Oh the glory of pure worship! His
being was controlled by the Spirit, and there was nothing fleshly about
his worship. This means he had moved out of his space into God's and
worship consumed his body, spirit, and soul. He was being governed
by the presence of God. Jesus said, **"But the time is coming—indeed
it's here now—when true worshippers will worship the Father in
spirit and in truth. The Father is looking for those who will worship
Him that way. For God is a Spirit, so those who worship Him must
worship in spirit and in truth"** (John 4:23-24 NLT).

One can be in worship but not in the spirit. John, being in the spirit in
worship, suggested that his worship was pure. It flowed from the truth
that was in his spirit. **"It was the Lord's Day, and I was worshipping**

in the Spirit" (Revelation 1:10 NLT). For worship to reach heaven, it must be in spirit and in truth. John was beyond the flesh and in the Spirit worshipping on the Lord's Day. He was experiencing pure worship, that deep level of worship where his spirit was drawn out of this sphere and given access to the glory hemisphere. It's that place in worship where your heart connects with the heart of God and you are consumed by His glory.

Oh that the people of God would take the time to worship Him in spirit and in truth! Worshipping in the Spirit is not just having a worship experience but the spirit of worship having you and you being enraptured by the power of worship. It's the worship of the saints that will usher in the power and the glory. It is always Satan's desire to keep us from pure worship so that there will be limited or no glory. But we as the people of God must push past the weight of Satan's lies to go from His presence into His power and glory. The church needs to experience the glory of worship!

John's physical condition and location did not hinder John's worship, for he knew where his help came from. His physical condition should have kept him from worship, but it pushed him into worship. He chose to worship in spite of his condition and had a glory encounter which would change his name to John the Revelator. When you choose to worship despite your physical condition, despite the persecution, sufferings, discomfort, and pain, something unusual happens. God shows up and neither you nor your situation remains the same. In the book of Job, Job refused to give in to his physical pain. In spite of all his sufferings, he chose to worship God. His worship ushered in the glory and the Lord restored his fortunes. The Bible says, "**In fact, the Lord gave him twice as much as before!**" (Job 42:10 NLT). When worship is for real, an everlasting change takes place, a supernatural change takes place, and you are transported to God's space. And there His glory is revealed.

John was worshipping on the Lord's Day. The Lord's Day was observed by the early church on Sunday because it was the day of Jesus' resurrection.

This does not take away from the strength of recognizing the seventh day of the week as the Sabbath but suggests to us that the first day was set aside by them as a day of thanksgiving, praise, and worship for all God had done.

The Sabbath

We could never preempt Saturday as the Sabbath. Yes, I know what Paul has to say in Colossians 2:16. **"So don't let anyone condemn you for what you eat or drink, or for not celebrating certain holy days or new moon ceremonies or Sabbaths."** He is not suggesting that we no longer need the Ten Commandments but saying that we are not bound to these holy days, new moon ceremonies, or Sabbaths. Jesus has set us free from legal and ceremonial obligations of this nature. **"But when the right time came, God sent His Son, born of a woman, subject to the law. God sent Him to buy freedom for us who were slaves to the law"** (Galatians 4:4-5a NLT).

The Sabbath day (a day of rest) was instituted by God in the book of Genesis. **"And God blessed the seventh day and declared it holy, because it was the day He rested from all His work of creation"** (Genesis 2:3). This suggests to us that from the time of creation, God wanted man to have a day of rest. This holy day was given to man by God long before the Jewish law. It was established as a day of blessing for everyone and not just for the Jewish race. This day of rest was given for our physical and spiritual well-being, and nowhere in Scriptures is it suggested that this God-given principle (that is needed to experience the abundant life) has been done away with. Jesus Himself spoke of the Sabbath as a gift of God to man. **"The Sabbath was made to meet the needs of the people, and not people to meet the requirements of the Sabbath. So the Son of Man is Lord, even over the Sabbath!"** (Mark 2:27-27 NLT).

The Sabbath should always prepare us for a glory experience on the Lord's Day. It's a day of restoration, both physically and spiritually, after completing five days of physical labor. Our bodies and spirit man need the Sabbath rest to complete its seven-day cycle and enjoy the glory of life that God has given to us. When a believer takes full advantage of this blessed day, he or she is more prepared for worship on the Lord's Day and his or her body does not expire before its appointed time.

The Seven Golden Lampstands

"When I turned to see who was speaking to me, I saw seven gold lampstands" (Revelation 1:12 NLT). The seven gold lampstands refer to the seven churches to which the letters were addressed. The gold lampstands represent not only the seven churches in John's day but the church universal, the ecclesia, a people set apart for God's glory. The church is precious to God. Golden lampstands suggest something of great value. As believers, we are the church of the living God . . . the ecclesia, a kingdom of priests!

In Matthew 5:14, Jesus told His disciples that they were the light of the world. He is the originator of that light. The church is compared to lampstands because they hold forth the light of the world. We are the carriers of true light. Jesus spoke to the people and said, **"I am the light of the world. If you follow me, you won't have to walk in darkness, because you will have the light that leads to life"** (John 8:12 NLT). The church is the torchbearer of glory and truth. Believers are supposed to light up the world with God's glory and truth. Our lamps should burn brightly at all times, during every season of our lives.

As a Christian family, when our children were young we did a spiritual exercise during family devotions. We would ask the questions "How bright a light were you for Jesus today? Were you a bright light, a not too bright light, or a dim light?" The answers always brought either a level of joy or repentance from the family members. What would be your answers to these questions?

The Glorious Christ

"And standing in the middle of the lamp stands was someone like the Son of Man. He was wearing a long robe with a gold sash across His chest. His head and His hair were white like wool, as white as snow. And His eyes were like flames of fire. His feet were like polished bronze refined in a furnace, and His voice thundered like mighty ocean waves. He held seven stars in His right hand, and a sharp two-edged sword came from His mouth. And His face was like the sun in all its brilliance" (Revelation 1:13-16 NLT).

John saw Christ in all of His glory! He saw Him as King, Priest, and Judge of His church, and He was standing in the midst of the lampstands that represented his church. What a comforting thought, that Jesus is standing in the midst of His church, His ecclesia, His kingdom of priests! Jesus is forever present, always ready to help in times of trouble. **"God has put all things under the authority of Christ and has made Him Head over all things for the benefit of the Church"** (Ephesians 1:22 NLT).

This picture of Jesus standing in the midst of His church is a source of great encouragement. He is letting us know that what He said in Scriptures is true: He is always with us. **"Lo, I am with you even unto the end of the age"** (Matthew 18:20b NLT). He is saying to us today, "I am with you when the times are good, I am with you when the times are bad, I am with you when you are feeling sad, lo, I am with you!" What an empowering thought! Christ is always with us. His glorious presence is with His church. He is standing in the midst of His glorious church. We need not fear the fiery darts of the enemy because our refuge and strength is with us.

The next time you meet as His ecclesia, remember He is in our midst. We can't exclude His glorious presence from our coming together, but we should let the splendor of His presence be made visible and not allow man's wisdom to dominate. The little chorus says, "He is here alleluia, He is here Amen; He is here glory, glory, I can bless His name again.

He is here listen closely, hear him calling out your name. He is here you can touch Him, you will never be the same" (Kirk Talley and the Talley Trio, "He is Here"). Oh the glory of God's presence in our midst! When the church arises to embrace the glory of His presence, there will be glory manifestations (visibility of His power) in our services. The lame will walk, the dumb will talk, the blind will see, sicknesses and diseases will have to flee, and above all souls will be delivered and saved. He is here. Amen!

When the church comes together, we must recognize that Jesus holds the keys to every work of the Devil. His anointed presence will be manifested through signs and wonders. Nothing will be able to hold the church back from experiencing ever-increasing glory. It was through His blood that He purchased us and destroyed the works of the Devil. "**But the Son of God came to destroy the works of the devil**" (1 John 3:8 NLT). And He did! "**He canceled the record of the charges against us and took it away by nailing it to the cross. In this way, He disarmed the spiritual rulers and authorities. He shamed them publicly by His victory over them on the cross**" (Colossians 2:14-15 NLT).

John tried his best to describe the glorious presence of Jesus. Can you imagine seeing Jesus and then trying to describe what you saw? John saw the King of Glory robed in all His majesty.

1) **Son of Man**—John said He saw someone likened to the Son of Man. This suggests that He was manlike in His appearance. This was a title Jesus gave to Himself. "**For as Jonah was in the belly of the great fish for three days and three nights, so will the Son of man be in the heart of the earth for three days and three nights**" (Matthew 12:40 NLT). The Son of Man is standing in our midst at all times, and during each season of our lives . . . *this* is our peace. This is our joy! This is our glory!

2) **Clothed with a garment down to the foot**—John saw Him as the church's High Priest. He was clothed in His priestly attire—"**He has become our eternal High Priest in the order**

of **Melchizedek"** (Hebrews 6:20 NLT). **"So then, since we have a great High Priest who has believed"** (Hebrews 4:14 NLT). Jesus stands in the midst of His church as our High Priest, Our Chief Intercessor, our Mediator, our Reconciler. Oh the glory!

3) **"Girded about the breasts with a golden girdle"**—Symbol of absolute authority. This is a great reminder to us the church that Jesus has absolute authority over His ecclesia. He has also delegated His authority to the church and is standing in our midst, encouraging us to use it. **"I have been given all authority in heaven and on earth. Therefore, go and make disciples of all the nations, baptizing them in the name of the Father and the Son and the Holy Spirit. Teach these new disciples to obey all the commands I have given you. And be sure of this: I am with you always, even to the end of the age"** (Matthew 18-20 NLT). Jesus dwells among us—what an awesome truth! We don't have to be afraid or timid in running this race of faith. All that really matters is that we believe and exercise the authority that is ours through Jesus Christ.

4) **His head and His hair were as white as wool, as white as snow**—He was, He is, and He is to come. Daniel refers to Him as the Ancient One. He is from time immemorial. **"I watched as thrones were put in place and the Ancient One sat down to judge. His clothing was as white as snow, His hair like purest wool"** (Daniel 7:9 NLT). He is the righteous Judge. There is no limit to God's righteousness as is revealed through Jesus. It is from everlasting to everlasting even as He is from everlasting to everlasting.

5) **His eyes were like flames of fire**—God is love, but He is also a consuming fire. Disobedience to his Word will arouse the holy indignation of our God. We must not offend the glorious presence of God at anytime! He will not violate His holiness to accommodate us. **"Since we are receiving a kingdom**

that is unshakable, let us be thankful and please God by worshipping Him with holy fear and awe. For our God is a devouring fire" (Hebrews 12:28 NLT).

6) **His feet like fine bronze**—Judgment of God. Whenever the church is not what it should be, the presence of the Lord will judge it. The feet of the Lord will stamp out the evil among us. **"It is a terrible thing to fall into the hands of the living God"** (Hebrews 10:31 NLT). Let God be glorified and the enemy be horrified!

7) **His voice like the sound of many waters**—A day is coming when the voice of the Son of God will be heard above every other voice and all mankind will respond to the sound. **"The voice of the Lord echoes above the sea. The God of glory thunders. The Lord thunders over the mighty sea. The voice of the Lord is powerful; the voice of the Lord is majestic. The voice of the Lord splits the mighty cedars; He makes Lebanon Mountains skip like a calf; He makes Mount Hermon leap like a young wild ox. The voice of the Lord strikes with bolts of lightning . . . In His temple everyone shouts, GLORY!"** (Psalm 29:3-7; 9b NLT).

8) **In His right hand He held seven stars**—The seven stars represent the angels of the churches (Revelation 1:20). Who are the angels of the churches? There are two popular views. Some scholars believe that they are angels on assignment to guard the churches, while others believe that they are the pastors (spiritual leaders) or elders.[2] It is a comforting thought to know that God is holding the church leaders in His hand. The pastors are not leading on their own, but as He directs.

9) **Out of His mouth came a sharp doubled-edged sword**—The grace and judgment of God's Word. The two-edged sword

---

2   *Life Application Study Bible Commentary*, New Living Translation, p. 2170.

represents the Word of God, which shows forth the judgment of God and the grace of God. God's Word is used to cut away sin and offers pardon to the sinner. When sin and glory meet, judgment takes place. In Acts 5, Ananias and Sapphira tried to deceive God and His people. God's glory was present and they were judged. We must always remember that God will not violate His holiness to entertain sin.

When sin and grace meet, deliverance takes place. **"So if the Son sets you free, you are truly free"** (John 8:36 NLT). It is the word of God that makes His glory visible in the church. You cannot separate the glory from God's Word. You cannot separate God's Word from His presence. All of His glory is in His word . . . The more word that is active in the church; the more glory will be visible by all. **"For the word of God is alive and powerful. It is sharper than the sharpest two-edged sword, cutting between soul and spirit, between joint and marrow. It exposes our innermost thought and desires. Nothing in all creation is hidden from God. Everything is naked and exposed before His eyes, and He is the one to whom we are accountable"** (Hebrews 4:12-13 NLT).

10) **His face was like the sun in all its brilliance**—The glorified Christ. John saw Christ in all His glory. He was fully arrayed and His countenance shone like the sun in all its strength . . . *Oh the glory of His presence!* He saw him as Priest, King, and Judge standing in the midst of His church, holding the anointed and appointed leaders in His right hand and showing forth His strength through the power of His spoken word. **"He held seven stars in his right hand, and a sharp two-edged sword came from his mouth. And his face was like the sun in all its brilliance"** (Revelation 1:16 NLT).

Jesus is constantly standing in the midst of His church. You may not feel His glorious presence at times because of religion, tradition, and other ritualistic acts of worship, but He is there! When you follow the methodology of man rather than the truth of God's Word, we deny His manifested presence, but He is there! Your religious beliefs may cloud His presence, but He is there. When the church overcomes these religious demons, the power and glory of Jesus' presence will be revealed. His manifested glory will be experienced in our midst as the High Priest. **"But now Jesus, our High Priest, has been given a ministry that is far superior to the old priesthood, for he is the one who mediates for us a far better covenant with God, based on better promises"** (Hebrews 8:6 NLT). He is the promise keeper! We will experience His glory as our King. **"Open up, ancient gates! Open up, ancient doors, and let the King of glory enter"** (Psalm 24:9 NLT). He is the Lord of heaven's armies! And there will also be times we will face Him as judge. **"The Lord will judge his own people. It is a terrible thing to fall into the hands of the living God"** (Hebrews 10:30b; 11-31 NLT). What a mighty God we serve!

John was knocked lifeless by the revelation of the glorified Christ. He could not remain standing in the presence of such unveiled glory. He was overwhelmed by the brilliance of Jesus' splendor, which he said was like the sun in all its strength! Throughout Scriptures we see where the manifestation of God's glory demands worship.

On that great day of the Lord, saints and sinners alike will recognize the authority and rule of Jesus the Christ as the true Lamb of glory and as the Lion of the tribe of Judah! **"That at the name of Jesus every knee should bow, in heaven and on earth and under the earth, and every tongue confess that Jesus Christ is Lord, to the glory of God the Father"** (Philippians 2:10-11 NLT). **"I am the First and the Last. I am the living One. I died, but look—I am alive forever and ever! And I hold the keys of death and the grave"** (Revelation 1:17b-18 NLT). Jesus identifies Himself to John as the Ancient of Days—He was, He is, and He forevermore shall be. Jesus was before all things: "He was chosen before the creation of the world, but was revealed in these last times for your sake" (1Peter 1:20NIV). And He will be after all things: **"And He will reign forever and ever** (Revelation 11:15b NLT).

"Write down what you have seen, what is now and what will take place later" (Revelation 1:19 NIV). This is the key verse in the book of

Revelation that unlocks the door to the entire book and its outline: a) The former manifestation of God's glory (what John saw) (Revelation 1:1-18), b) The present manifestation of the glory (what is now) (Revelation 2 and 3), and c) the latter manifestation of the glory (that which will take place later) (Revelation 4:22).

The writing of this book is a full unveiling of God's glory. The power and glory of God are revealed in each chapter. It takes you from glory to glory. **"And we who with unveil faces all reflect the Lord's glory, are being transformed into His likeness with ever-increasing glory, which comes from the Lord, who is the Spirit"** (2 Corinthians 3:18 NIV).

QUESTIONS FOR REVIEW

1. How many lampstands were there and what did they represent?

2. What is the meaning of ecclesia?

3. Can you describe the Son of Man as John saw Him in verses 13-15 of this first chapter?

4. Explain the title Son of Man.

5. What is Jesus' ministry as our High Priest?

6. How limited is the righteousness of God?

7. What will be the attitude of God's judgment on the day of the Lord?

8. What does the double-edged sword represent?

9. Which verse is the key verse to the book of Revelation and why?

10. Have you ever experienced the power and glory of worship? Expound

CHAPTER THREE

Message to the Seven Churches

Revelation 2 and 3

Message to the Seven Churches

The letters in the book of Revelation were written to the angels (leaders) of the churches in Asia Minor: Ephesus, Smyrna, Pergamum, Thyatira, Sardis, Philadelphia, and Laodicea. They were actual churches in John's day. These seven letters to the churches are just as important to us, the church today, as they were in John's day. The Word of God is continually examining, correcting, and probing the heart of His church.

Why these seven churches were chosen from among the hundreds of churches located in cities all over the world by this time (some sixty-three years after Pentecost) is not known. It is believed that the seven churches represent the seven basic division of church history (the church has gone through seven periods or stages). But Jesus chooses these seven and their spiritual condition speaks of churches throughout all generations.

The letters reveals what Jesus loves and values in His church and what He hates and condemns. It also reveals the consequences of disobedience and spiritual neglect. The church must constantly show forth the glory of God among men. We must not be negligent concerning spiritual matters. When we are in sin and are not functioning under the weight of God's glory, Jesus speaks to us from the glory so that we may once again function on the earth as His glory vessels.

As God's ecclesia, our mandate is to show forth His glory. There is to be ever-increasing glory in God's church. We are to advance farther and farther into God's glorious presence through pure prayer, fasting, the study of God's Word, fellowship with other believers, thanksgiving, praise, and worship. His Spirit of truth, holiness, and righteousness should govern the atmosphere of our lives and the life of His church. We will experience glory rain in the church when we the believers meet the requirements of heaven.

Always remember that Jesus is forever standing in the midst of His church and He is holding the leaders in His right hand. We are also to remember that because He is forever present, His word and great grace and mercy are forever present. The two-edged sword never leaves the mouth of Christ. His word will commend us or condemn us. It will commend us for our righteousness (obedience) and will challenge us. But it will also condemn us for our sins and resistance to His will. His grace and mercy will continually restore and deliver us from the judgment of God.

God does not only want His church to talk about His power and glory, but He wants His church to be the demonstration of His power and glory on the earth. He wants us to live in the center of His glory. As believers, whatever we do in thought, word, or deed should bring glory to the Father. Even now He is speaking to His church and admonishing us to stop the excessive talking and get into Him that there may be demonstrations of His power and glory! **"For the kingdom of God is not just a lot of talk; it is living by God's power"** (1 Corinthians 4:20 NLT).

The church was founded by Jesus Christ. **"Now I say to you that you are Peter, and upon this rock, I will build my Church, and all the powers of hell will not conquer it"** (Matthew 16:18 NLT). Jesus was placed in charge of everything pertaining to the church. **"God has put all things under the authority of Christ and has made Him head over all things for the benefit of the Church"** (Ephesians 1:22 NLT). Jesus introduced himself to the church by going back to the vision of Himself that was given to John in chapter 1 and uses one of the characteristics of His glorious nature in His letter to each of the churches.

Ephesus—The One who holds the seven stars in His right hand; the One who walks in the midst of the seven gold lampstands.

Smyrna—The First and the Last, who was dead but is now alive.

Pergamum—The One with the sharp two-edged sword.

Thyatira—The One whose eyes are like flames of fire, whose feet are like polished bronze.

Sardis—The One who has the sevenfold Spirit of God and the seven stars.

Philadelphia—The One who is holy and true, the One who has the key of David.

Laodicea—The One who is the amen—the faithful and true witness, the beginning of God's new creation.

Ephesus—Apostolic Church

"Write this letter to the angel of the church in Ephesus. This is the message from the One who holds the seven stars in His right hand, the One who walks among the seven gold lampstands" (Revelation 2:1 NLT). The church at Ephesus was founded by Paul along with Priscilla and Aquilla during his second missionary journey. It was known for its vibrant and evangelistic ministries. The glory of God certainly seemed to have been visible in this congregation.

In Paul's letter to this church, he talked about their great love for God's people and their enduring faith. **"Ever since I first heard of your strong faith in the Lord Jesus and your love for God's people everywhere"** (Ephesians 1:15-16 NLT). This commendation by Paul was some thirty years before this letter was given to John. Ephesus was known as a church of excellence, a working church that stood strong in the word of God and exercised great faith.

Jesus' commendation for the church was great. **"I know all the things you do. I have seen your hard work and your patient endurance. I know you don't tolerate evil people. You have examined the claims of those who say they are apostles but are not. You have discovered they are liars. You have patiently suffered for me without quitting"** (Revelation 2-3 NLT). What words of commendation from the lips of Jesus!

He praised the church for its excellent standard in holiness. This was a working church that was persistent and patient. It seemed to have been very thorough in what its members believed. They were doctrinally sound, knew the Word, and used it. We can be true to our churches but not true to our God because our commitment to our church can be greater than our commitment to God.

This church was situated in a city that was known for its wickedness and worship of the goddess Diana. This was a working church that hated the deeds of immoral Nicolaitans (believers who did not compromised their faith in order to enjoy some of the sinful practices of Ephesus). There was visible glory in the church, but the glory was not governing the church's atmosphere. Many churches have limited glory. God wants us to get to the place where the glory envelops us and there are no limits but riveting glory in every season. But after Jesus' great commendation, He had a grave complaint against this church. Yes, they were commended for their hard work and patient endurance, but Jesus found them lacking in the most important ingredient of any church.

"But I have this complaint against you. You don't love me or each other as you did at first! Look how far you have fallen!" (Revelation 2:4-5 NLT). As Jesus stood in the midst of the seven golden lampstands, He examined them, walked among them, and lodged a complaint against them. The church of Ephesus was lacking in love. The love for God and each other had grown cold. Whenever Jesus has a complaint against His body, there will always be limited glory. **"You don't love me or each other as you did at first,"** he said. Where there is a lack of love, there will be a lack of glory; love is the key to the greater glory. A church with little love is a church with little glory; love is the presence of glory. The church was too busy doing for God and had no time to be with God. There was no deep intimacy with Christ.

The church had lost its sparkle, passion for God. They were no longer excited about their faith, the thrill was gone, and their love for God and each other had dried up. They were still busy serving God, but their love had dried up. Their motive in service was not born out of a heart of love. Here was a church clothed in doctrinal purity but naked in love. Here was a church still teaching and preaching against evil but its love for God, its desire for His glorious presence had grown cold. His glory was not visible among its members. They had the form of Jesus but not the power and glory. They were warned by Jesus to return to the glory.

"Turn back to me and do the works you did at first, if you don't repent, I will come and remove your lampstand from its place among the churches" (Revelation 2:5 NLT). Jesus' instructions to the church in Ephesus were to repent and begin to love like they did at first. Clothe yourself once again in the love of God and allow love to govern your life, He was saying to them. "Love me like you did at first. Love your neighbor like you did at first. Serve me like you did at first. Serve your neighbor like you did at first." Jesus warned them that if true repentance did not take place, their lampstand would be removed from its place. If the lampstands were removed, there would be no glory covering in the church. Jesus would no longer stand or walk in their presence; He would remove their lampstand from His glorious presence.

Overcomer's Reward

"To Him who overcomes, I will give the right to eat from the Tree of Life, which is in the paradise of God" (Revelation 2:7 NIV). Jesus' overcomer's reward to the church in Ephesus is that they will be given the right to eat from the Tree of Life, which is in God's Paradise (garden). Overcomers are ones who remain constant in the faith and is victorious over the world, the flesh, and the Devil. They are the committed ones who refuse to compromise their love for God. They are the constant seekers of his glory, not His gifts. Their desire is to please God and God alone without being easily offended by others. They never feel the need to quit. They never give up. They are the press-alongers of the faith who endure to the very end.

What did Ephesus have to overcome? Ephesus's problem was a lack of love for God and each other. They were rendering lip service and not heart service to God. The church was challenged to get up and begin to demonstrate love toward God and each other by honoring God's Word. Their way of worship was not enough because it was impure. Their lack of love for God and each other made it impure. There was very little glory in their worship. There was very little passion for God. When our worship is for real, the love of God, the love for God and each other, will flow through our worship experience. A glorified church is governed by the love of God.

Smyrna—The Persecuted Church

"I know about your suffering and your poverty—but you are rich! I know the blasphemy of those opposing you. They say they are Jews, but they are not, because their synagogue belongs to Satan" (Revelation 2:9 NLT). This is the shortest letter of the seven that were written. Smyrna suffered much persecution but remained faithful. It is said of the early church that they were marked by their material poverty and spiritual power. Today's church is marked by its material wealth and spiritual weakness. The material wealth has taken the place of God in many of our modern-day churches. We worship the mighty dollar and not the mighty God. Smyrna was just the opposite. They had very little of this world's wealth but were heavily laden with heaven's wealth.

There is no condemnation of Smyrna. This church suffered much for the glory of God and, although greatly opposed for their faith, they remained strong. They were surrounded by physical and material poverty, yet Jesus said they were rich! Theirs was a church filled with spiritual millionaires. They had it going on in the glory of God! In being that glorified church, there are the times when you will appear to be poor, but those are the times when you are a true millionaire in the Spirit. **"Our hearts ache, but we always have joy. We are poor, but we give spiritual riches to others. We own nothing, and yet we have everything"** (2 Corinthians 6:10 NLT).

"Don't be afraid of what you are about to suffer. The devil will throw some of you into prison to test you. You will suffer for ten days. But if you remain faithful even when facing death, I will give you the crown of life" (Revelation 2:10 NLT). Jesus told the church in Smyrna not to be afraid of the upcoming suffering because it would only be a test which will have temporary lasting strength and no enduring power. The Devil would not be able to prevail in his attack against them. Always remember that suffering won't last forever. It has a beginning and an end. Their faithfulness even at the point of death will produce a greater glory for the kingdom of God and a greater reward for the child of God. **"But if you remain faithful even when facing death, I will give you the crown of life."**

What a reward for the faithful child of God! The crown of life, the victor's wreath, will be theirs. All of the life of God will be theirs for all eternity! **"God blesses you when people mock you and persecute you and lie about you and say all sorts of evil things against you because you are my followers. Be happy about it! Be very glad! For a great reward awaits you in heaven. And remember, the ancient prophets were persecuted in the same way"** (Matthew 5:11-12 NLT). As the church, we need to run and not look back, press onward and not give up.

We have been promised a crown of life . . . not a perishable crown but an imperishable one, a glory crown. Keep running and keep pressing! The best is yet to come!

Overcomer's Reward

"Whoever is victorious will not be hurt by the second death" (Revelation 2:11b NLT). Only the faithful overcomers will escape the second death (the lake of fire). Smyrna's challenge was to continue to overcome the persecution and trial that they were going through. They were encouraged to keep on running the race of faith and to remain faithful even to the point of death. Even now Jesus is speaking to His church, encouraging them to go through their trials and persecution knowing that it does not have the strength to last forever; nor can it destroy a faithful, righteous seed . . . Go through!

Pergamum—The Liberal Church

"I know you live in a city where Satan has his throne, yet you have remained loyal to me. You refused to deny me even when Antipas, my faithful witness, was martyred among you there in Satan's city" (Revelation 2:13 NLT). It was not easy to be a Christian in this city. It was the center of four cults and was second only to Ephesus in idol worship. Jesus called it Satan's city. As a believer, don't you feel at times that you are living in Satan's city? There is so much horrendous crime and evil lurking all around our cities. The church's cry must constantly be for the glory of God to be revealed and the powers of darkness destroyed over our land. Pergamum was a sophisticated city. A city of the learned where there was a great influence of satanic activities. Jesus commended them for remaining true to His name in the midst of the evil. Even in the face of death, they refused to renounce their faith in His name. May we the church of today, even in the face of death, refuse to renounce our faith in God.

"But I have a few complaints against you. You tolerate some among you whose teaching is like that of Balaam, who showed Balak how to trip up the people of Israel. He taught them to sin by eating food offered to idols and by committing sexual sin. In a similar way, you have some Nicolaitans among you who follow the same teaching" (Revelation 2:14 NLT). After such commendation, you would not expect there to be such a harsh rebuke! In the midst of holding fast to the name of Christ, the church in Pergamum allowed pagan immorality to slip in and contaminate them; they tolerated Balaam's doctrine. Like Balaam, there were those among them who did religious work for personal gain. Their focus was not on the glory but on their personal interests, which resulted in them teaching a compromising faith, leading to the teaching of false doctrine. The teachers not only were among them, but Jesus said that they were tolerated by the church.

"Repent of your sin, or I will come to you suddenly and fight against them with the sword of my mouth" (Revelation 2:15-16 NLT). Jesus told the church to repent or there would be a sudden fight against them. The sword of His mouth is His word. His very word would fight against them unless they repented and became free from compromising teachers and preachers. Holiness is still God's way for His church. It must remain a glorified body at all times, hating the sin and loving the sinner.

The Word of God will fight against any church that has a tolerant attitude toward sin. "Oh, the joys of those who do not follow the advice of the wicked, or stand around with sinners, or join in with mockers. But they delight in the law of the Lord, meditating on it day and night" (Psalm 1:1-2 NLT). As the church, let us hold fast to our faith and not be found by Jesus to be in any compromising position.

Overcomer's Reward

"To him that overcomes, I will give some of the hidden manna. I will also give him a white stone with a new name written on it, known only to him who receives it" (Revelation 2:17 NIV). This church had to overcome the power of sin that lived in its midst. The church was told that if they overcame the sin around them and quit their tolerance of false teachers and preachers, they would be given some of the hidden manna and a white stone with a new name known only to the one who received it. The hidden manna is the nourishment of all the faithful believers, and the white stone can be called "the stone of Acquittal." It is symbolic of our eternal acquittal through Jesus Christ's blood. Every faithful believer will have a new name that will be written through the blood. May we hold fast to our faith and not be overcome by the evil around us, but let us overcome the evil!

Thyatira—The Church of the Dark Age

"I know all the things you do. I have seen your love, your faith, your service, and your patient endurance. And I can see your constant improvement in all these things" (Revelation 2:19 NLT). Here was a city without focus on any particular religion. Thyatira was a secular and wealthy city in Macedonia known for its trades. It is believed that the city was converted by Lydia. "One of them was Lydia from Thyatira, a merchant of expensive purple cloth, who worshipped God. As she listened to us, the Lord opened her heart, and she accepted what Paul was saying" (Acts 16:14 NLT). Jesus commends this church for its works, love, service, faith, and patient endurance. Here was a church that was growing in the ways of the Lord and experiencing increasing glory. Jesus told the church He was able to see their constant improvement in all these things.

"But I have this complaint against you. You are permitting that woman—that Jezebel who calls herself a prophet—to lead my servants astray. She teaches them to commit sexual sin and to eat food offered to idols. I gave her time to repent, but she does not want to turn away from her immorality" (Revelation 2:20-21 NLT). Although there was constant improvement in the spiritual life of the church, there was also a strong complaint by Jesus against this church. They had a tendency to tolerate unrighteousness and ungodly teaching from some of its leaders. Jesus refers to one of the leaders as Jezebel.

The name Jezebel may have been used to symbolize the graveness of the evil. In Old Testament times, Jezebel was the name of a pagan queen who persuaded her husband King Ahab to sin against God. This New Testament Jezebel taught that immorality was a serious matter for believers. Jesus said that he had given her time to repent, but she refused to turn away from her immoral lifestyle.

"But I also have a message for the rest of you in Thyatira who have not followed this false teaching (deeper truths as they call them—depths of Satan, actually). I will ask nothing more of you except that you hold tightly to what you have until I come" (Revelation 2:24-25 NLT). Jesus had a message for those who had held on to their faith in spite of the false teaching around them. He encouraged them to remain faithful until His return.

Overcomer's reward

"To him who overcomes and does my will to the end, I will give authority over the nations—He will rule them with an iron scepter; he will dash them to pieces like pottery just as I have received authority from my Father. I will also give Him the morning star" (Revelation 2:26-28 NLT). The overcomer will be given a position of leadership and authority during the millennial age. They will reign with Jesus. The morning star represents Christ's glorious abiding presence with the overcomer. The morning star appears just before the dawn, when the night is cold and dark. Our morning star appears to us when we are at our worst and our nights seem endless. He comes with overwhelming joy, overwhelming peace, and overwhelming glory! **"Weeping may last through the night, but joy comes with the morning"** (Psalm 30:5b NLT).

Sardis—The Dead Church

Sardis was a very wealthy city. It was the capital city of Lydia and was prominent in Asia Minor. Sardis was known for its carpet making and was destroyed by an earthquake. **"I know all the things you do, and that you have a reputation for being alive—but you are dead"** (Revelation 3:1 NLT). This church received no commendation from Jesus. "**I know all the things you do.**" Is it really a commendation? The church at Sardis was pronounced by Jesus to be dead! There was no spiritual life in this church; the glory had departed, and they were spiritually dead.

"You have a reputation for being alive—but you are dead." Sardis had a reputation for being alive, but it was dead! The life of Jesus was not in the church. They had the form of glory, but not the power. They still praised and worshipped God but not in spirit and in truth. They looked good from the outside, but Jesus was dealing with the inside. God is a heart God! We can look good from the outside, but what is happening on the inside? The power of life lies within and is demonstrated without. It was a religious church and not a spiritual church. It was a dead church with no spiritual life.

"Wake up! Strengthen what little remains, for even what is left is almost dead. I find that your actions do not meet the requirements of my God. Go back to what you heard and believed at first; hold to it firmly. Repent and turn to Me again. If you don't wake up, I will come to you suddenly, as unexpected as a thief" (Revelation 3:2-3 NLT). Jesus warned the church to wake up from its spiritual slumber and to strengthen what remained. Even the little that remained was dying. **"For even what is left is almost dead."**

Their deeds were offensive to God. Jesus counseled them to go back to what they heard and believed at first and to hold fast to it. The church can become full of religion and not full of the glory if we are not spending time with God in prayer and fasting. Holding fast to our faith is the key to spiritual success. **"Repent and turn to me again. If you don't wake up, I will come to you suddenly, as unexpected as a thief."** Jesus counsels the church to get rid of religion and begin to seek Him. If true repentance did not take place, they would experience the judgment of God.

"Yet there are some in the Church in Sardis who have not soiled their clothes with evil." There were the believers who refused to compromise their faith and continued being seekers of His true glory. Those who refused to be contaminated by evil dressed up in the name of religion. "They will walk with me in white, for they are worthy." The remnant (those who hold fast to holiness) will be the ones who experience God's glory.

Overcomer's Reward

"He who overcomes will, like them, be dressed in white. I will never blot out His name from the book of life, but will acknowledge his name before my Father and His angels" (Revelation 3:5 NIV). Here is a verse of Scripture that was given to us by Jesus. It tells us there will be members of the body of Christ whose names will be blotted out of the Book of Life if they fall away from the faith.

Jesus' promise to the overcomers was that like the remnant: they would be dressed in white and their names will not be blotted out of the Book of Life, but that He will announce to the Father and His angels that they are His!

Philadelphia—The Alive Church

"I know all the things you do, and I have opened a door for you that no one can close. You have little strength, yet you obeyed my word and did not deny me" (Revelation 3:8 NLT). Like the church at Smyrna, there was no condemnation. Oh to God that all of His church would desire to be like the church in Smyrna and Philadelphia! Their story was truly for God's glory. This was the true church of the Living God. Jesus commended them for keeping His word and not denying Him. They had come up against great opposition from the world and were able to resist the power of wickedness at every level.

They were strong in the faith and remained steadfast and loyal to the cross of Jesus. **"Look, I will force those who belong to Satan's synagogue—those liars who say they are Jews but are not—to come and bow down at your feet. They will acknowledge that you are the ones I love"** (Revelation 3:9 NLT). Because of their overcoming faith, Jesus promised deliverance from their hour of trial. Jesus will always deliver a faithful church during their hour of trial. A faithful church is backed (supported) by all of God's Word and will never be overcome by evil. **"Upon this rock I will build my Church, and all the powers of hell will not overcome it"** (Matthew 16:18b NLT).

"Because you have obeyed my command to persevere, I will protect you from the great time of testing that will come upon the whole world to test those who belong to this world. I am coming soon. Hold on to what you have, so that no one will take away your crown" (Revelation 3:10-11 NLT). Jesus promises to protect His glorified church from the period of the great tribulation. There is always a blessing awaiting the obedient servants of God, so that during the times of great struggles and hard testing His Word will build a hedge of protection around about them. The promise to the church in Philadelphia was that the faithful believers would be raptured, taken out of this world before the great time of testing.

Overcomer's Reward

"Him who overcomes I will make a pillar in the temple of my God. Never again will he leave it. I will write on him the name of my God and the name of the city of my God, the new Jerusalem, which is coming down out of heaven from my God; and I will also write on him my new name" (Revelation 3:12 NIV).

The overcomer's reward is threefold.

1. He will be made a pillar in the temple of God and he will forever abide in the presence of the Lord.

2. He will have written on him the name of God and the name of the city of God. He will be forever God's masterpiece.

3. Christ will give him a new name and he will be rewarded for overcoming the world, flesh, and the Devil for the glory of God. Oh that we all would overcome!

Laodicea—The Contemporary or People's Church

"I know all the things you do, that you are neither hot nor cold. I wish that you were one or the other!" (Revelation 3:15 NLT). Like the church at Sardis, Jesus had no commendation, no note of praise for this church. What a sad commentary! When Jesus was walking in the midst of His church, He could find no note of praise, nothing that was pleasing. It was sickeningly lukewarm. Laodicea was the wealthiest of the seven cities. It was known for its manufacture of wool, a medical school that produced eye ointment, and its banking industry. Jesus compares their spiritual condition to lukewarm water, which they could identify with. The city of Laodicea once had an aqueduct built to bring water to the city from hot springs, and by the time the water reached the city it was neither hot nor cold but tepid (disgustingly) lukewarm.

Tim LaHaye in his book on Revelation says, "Our Lord makes clear that He is fully aware of the neutral condition of the church in the last days. It was not 'hot,' meaning 'zealous of good works,' nor was it 'cold,' meaning 'lifeless.' Instead it was 'lukewarm' or indifferent. What a description of the modern-day church! All kinds of organizations, programs, committees, activities, but no power."[3] He went on to say, "These churches are more interested in social action than gospel action, in reformation rather than transformation, in planning than praying."[4]

---

[3] Tim LaHaye, *Revelation Illustrated and Made Plain* (Zondervan Publishing House, 1975), p. 62.

[4] Ibid., p. 62.

Laodicea was also more interested in popularity rather than spirituality. Doesn't it sound a lot like the church of today? Sickeningly lukewarm! **"But since you are like lukewarm water, neither hot nor cold, I will spit you out of my mouth! You say, I am rich. I have everything I want. I don't need a thing! And you don't realize that you are wretched and miserable and poor and blind and naked"** (Revelation 3:16-17 NLT). The true state of the church in Laodicea was that it was lukewarm, wretched, miserable, poor, blind, and naked. This is what Jesus said concerning the Laodicean church. What is Jesus saying concerning your place of worship?

The church was wretched and miserable—They had become too modernized to be spiritualized. They had lessons on positive thinking rather than godly living. God's pulpit must be filled with Christ's word and soul-saving truth teaching and not man's philosophy, which is flesh pleasing. Motivational speakers will give you half-truths which feed your soul but not your spirit. They tell you what is needed to make you feel good but not what you need to keep you pure. Their teaching places no holy demands upon your love for God. It is more mind over matter and not mind given over to God.

The church was poor—They had an abundance of material wealth but no abundance of spiritual wealth. Their material prosperity had become more important to them than their spiritual well-being. Their focus was on earthly gain rather than heaven's gain. They were so wrapped up in material things that they did not recognize their spiritual condition. Material wealth is temporal and does not last forever. Spiritual wealth is eternal and will endure the test of time. They were materially comfortable and were blinded to the fact that they were spiritually wretched. Their wealth was giving them a false sense of comfort. **"So I advise you to buy gold from me—gold that has been purified by fire. Then you will be rich"** (Revelation 3:18 NLT). Christ advised the church to seek Him. It is in the seeking of Him that true riches can be found. **"Seek the kingdom of God above all else, and live righteously, and He will give you everything you need"** (Matthew 6:33 NLT).

The church was blind—They thought they knew the truth, but they did not understand the ways of God. They were blinded by their religious condition. Jesus told them to buy **"ointment for your eyes so you will be able to see"** (Revelation 3:18 NLT). Christ advised the church to get medicine from Him to heal their blindness. This is something the churches today are in dire need of: ointment for our spiritual eyes. We are in a state of blindness to spiritual matters and are not aware of it. We have been taken over by a spirit of complacency, and mediocrity and religiosity. Oh to God that we would receive this medicine! We need our spiritual eyes anointed!

The church was naked—The church was naked but did not see this because of the religious garb. They had the form, the appearance, of godliness but were powerless. They were still doing the things of God, but there was no presence of God. Their worship was merely a ritualistic act—no righteousness and no holiness thus no power and glory. This was a compromising church that felt like it had to change with the times rather than with the Word of God. **"Also buy white garments from me so you will not be shamed by your nakedness"** (Revelation 3:18a NLT). Jesus advised them to buy white garments from Him, which represented the righteousness of God. The glory will only be seen in the church when we are clothed in the righteousness of God and not our own righteousness. It is the righteous ones who will shine like the sun in the kingdom of God. **"Then the righteous will shine like the sun in the kingdom of their Father"** (Matthew 18:43 NIV). **"I correct and discipline everyone I love. So be diligent and turn from your indifference"** (Revelation 3:19 NLT). Jesus challenged the church to accept His loving discipline, be diligent, and repent.

Overcomer's Reward

"To him who overcomes, I will give the right to sit with me on my throne, just as I overcame and sat down with my father on His throne" (Revelation 3:21 NIV). The reward for overcoming this spirit of lukewarmness is to sit with Christ on His throne. **"Look! I stand at**

the door and knock. If you hear my voice and open the door, I will come in, and we will share a meal together as friends" (verse 20 NLT). The church in Laodicea had locked the Spirit of Christ out of the church. They had man-made programs and order but no God-approved agenda. It was God's house, a church that God had built, but His presence was not welcome. Christ challenged them to let His glorious presence come in. He is patient and persistent and will not force Himself in but continually waits.

Conclusion

To which church do you belong? Every church beside Sardis (dead church) and Laodicea (lukewarm church) had some commendation, some note of praise from Christ. All of the churches, with the exception of Smyrna (persecuted and suffering church) and Philadelphia (righteous, the alive church) had condemnations from Christ. Can you find your church (individually and collectively) among the letters?

Are you a true worshipper, a seeker of God's glory? Is your heart's door open to Christ who walks among the candlesticks? Is He the center of your joy? Are you a tepid (lukewarm) church? He is standing at your heart's door and knocking. Will you let him in? **"Look! I stand at the door and knock. If you hear my voice and open the door, I will come in, and we will share a meal together as friends"** (Revelation 3:20 NLT).

A Rhema Word for the Church
"Repent While There Is Still Time!"

The condition of the seven churches in this passage of Revelation speaks to the state of the church today. We are void of God's power and glory. We lack the fullness of His joy in our meetings and lives. There is very little hunger and thirst after His way of living. There is more flesh than Spirit. There are more hirelings than servants. There is more head knowledge than spiritual knowledge. The Spirit is saying,

1. "Repent! I have this complaint against you. You have left your first love. You are no longer committed to the way of truth. You're still shouting and praising, but your love for me and each other has grown cold. You are still working for me, but very little time is being spent with me. Remember how you used to worship and adore me? I was your all in all. What has happened to cause our relationship to be so casual? Repent therefore from where you have fallen. Repent and come back to me and love me like you did at first!"

2. "Repent! I have this complaint against you. You are polluted socially and spiritually. There is very little truth in your worship of me. There is too much of you in the teaching of my gospel. You must decrease. Your focus must be on me and not your achievements. You must allow my Spirit to increase in your life. Make room for the demonstration of heaven's power to flow through the life of the church. Stop trying to come up against me with contaminated worship. You must repent or be judged by my word!"

3. "Repent! I have this complaint against you. You have allowed the spirit of Jezebel who calls herself a prophetess to teach and seduce my servants to accepting the way of the world, holding on to contrary teachings. You have allowed my word to be

turned upside down in the life of my church by calling wrong right and right wrong. What a spiritual mess you have created! I have given you plenty of opportunities to repent, yet you would not. You need to stop right where you are and repent while there is yet time!"

4. "Repent! I have this complaint against you. What a great pretender you are! You have a name that says you are alive, but you are dead. The life of God no longer dwells among you. You have set yourself up as God in the house of the Lord. My people are drawn to you rather than to me. Their loyalty is to you rather than the God in you. You need to get up and turn your heart toward me once again and strengthen the things that remain. Hold fast to what is right and repent! Do it now or I will remove your candlestick!"

5. "Repent! I have these complaints against you. You are lukewarm. You want my blessings, but you do not want my glory. You do not want an intimate relationship with me the Blessor. You are more interested in social action than gospel action. You are more interested in reformation than transformation. You are more interested in planning than praying.[5] As my special possession, you say of yourself that you are rich and increased with goods and have need of nothing, but material abundance does not contribute to spiritual vitality. You are deathly ill and do not know it!"

6. "You are wretched, naked, and miserable. You deceive yourself! You are poor even though rich in material things because you know not Christ in His righteousness. You are blind although you claim to be learned because you do not understand and follow the ways of God in spirit and in truth. You do not know the true message of the cross. You have taken to man-made

5   Tim LaHaye, *Revelation Illustrated and Made Plain* (Grand Rapid Michigan: Zondervan Publishing House, 1975), p. 62.

doctrine and philosophy. You have trampled upon that which is sacred and have not acknowledged the power and presence of God. There is no reverence for God in your worship.

"Man can organize, man can build, and man can promote. Man can preach. Man can teach. But only My Spirit can convict and set free the souls of man. Only My Spirit can transform their lives[6] and bring glory to Christ in the church. Repent! Come and buy of me gold tried in the fire. Come and buy of me white raiment and anoint your eyes with salve that you may see my ever-increasing glory. The time of repentance is now for my power and glory must fill the earth.

"You must take your eyes of man and his accomplishments and seek God in all His glory. Be zealous and return to Me, your first love; love me as you did before. This is your hour to arise from your spiritually sick condition. I am at your heart door, knocking. Stop being a busybody and be a glory body. Why won't you listen and open the door? I want to come in and fellowship with you. I want to come in and empower you. I want to come in and dress you. I want to come in and use you. I want to come in and possess you, allow my river to flow through you. Let me show you my glory. Receive my glory. Repent! And come away in my power and glory."

---

[6]   Tim LaHaye, *Revelation Illustrated and Made Plain* (Grand Rapids Michigan: Zondervan Publishing, 1965), p. 63.

QUESTIONS FOR REVIEW

1. What do the letters to the seven churches reveal?

2. How did Jesus introduce Himself to each church?

3. What was Jesus' commendation to each church?

4. What was his condemnation to each church?

5. How were they challenged and what is the overcomer's reward?

6. How many churches received no condemnation? Why?

7. If Jesus was writing a letter to your church, what would it say?

CHAPTER FOUR

The Rapture of the Church

Revelation 4

We are in a season of ever-increasing glory and the church of God is moving deeper and deeper into the greater hemisphere of glory. God is raising up leaders who are committed to humbly seek His face and will take the time to ascend the hill of the Lord in prayer and worship. They, like Moses, are being clothed in the presence of the Lord. Through them the abundance of His presence will usher in this latter glory that will fill this earth and His glorious kingdom will be established. "**Thy kingdom come; thy will be done in earth, as it is in heaven**" (Matthew 6:10 KJV).

These spirit-filled leaders are the ones who are being used by God to orchestrate His story on the earth. They are a part of heaven's glory story. Their lives have been given over to God to be used for His glory. They are sold out to God and have no hidden agenda. These spiritual leaders are not after fame or fortune but rather the glory. They are the ones who are crying out for the church to get past denominational reign and religion and ritualistic acts (man's ways and order of things) so that the glorious presence of Jesus may once again govern His sanctuary. They press hard after the glorious presence of God and are hungry for a greater taste of His glory, and their eyes are fastened on Him through

His Holy Spirit. They are pliable in the hands of God and want nothing more than to be used by Him.

"Then as I looked, I saw a door standing open in heaven, and the same voice I had heard before spoke to me like a trumpet blast. The voice said, 'Come up here, and I will show you what must happen after this'" (Revelation 4:1 NLT). Most Bible scholars believe that this portion of Revelation is about things that will happen after the rapture of the church and that John being caught up into heaven is symbolic of the church being caught up . . . raptured from the earth.

The faithful ones of Christ's church, the ecclesia, will one day be caught up by Him; the letters to the churches were to prepare them for this great day. After chapter 3, the word *church* is never mentioned again until chapter 22. **"I, Jesus, have sent my angel to give you this message for the churches"** (Revelation 22:16 NLT). Therefore it is believed that the church is already in heaven before Jesus' return to earth in judgment of the wicked and to reign in the millennial kingdom. God sending Jesus for his bride (the church), His rich and glorious inheritance before the season of great judgment of the wicked, is an act of grace and mercy too great to fathom!

The word *rapture* is never mentioned in Scriptures. It is derived from the Latin word *raptus,* which means to "seize by force." The phrase *caught up* is a translation of the Greek word meaning to seize as a robber seizes his prize. One day Christ is coming to seize forcibly from this world His jewels—the ready believers who have kept faith alive. It will be a sudden snatching of His ready church out of the world. The Bible says it will happen in a moment in the twinkling of an eye. That's how suddenly it will take place.

This is the blessed hope of every believer, the reason for our faith and why we never give up but keep on fighting this great fight of faith! It is a win-win battle that we, God's faithful believers, are engaged in. We know that one day Jesus will return in the air and we will be snatched out of this wicked world by force. Think about it, saints: what glory it will be when Christ Jesus returns for His church! We will be caught up by the King of Glory into the glory forever.

I choose to highlight the word *ecclesia* at times rather than *church* to give clarity to the reader that Jesus' return will not be for a group of religious people we call the church but for a people who are set apart and known as the ecclesia—also known in the kingdom of God as the church (sanctified believers). It is the ecclesia (that set-apart body) that will be that glorious church without spot or wrinkle that will be seized by Jesus out of this world and into the next. **"We tell you this directly from the Lord. We who are still living when the Lord returns will not meet Him ahead of those who have died. For the Lord Himself will come down from heaven with a commanding shout, with the voice of the archangel, and with the trumpet call of God. First, the Christians who have died will rise from their graves, then, together with them, we who are still alive and remain on the earth will be caught up in the clouds to meet the Lord in the air. Then we will be with the Lord forever. So encourage each other with these words"** (1 Thessalonians 4:15-18 NLT).

Jesus' descent will be only for His bride, the ready church (His ecclesia) to ascend with Him. Every ready believer will be caught up to meet him in the air. **"You also must be ready all the time, for the Son of Man will come when least expected"** (Luke 12:40 NLT). Both the ready and the resurrected believers will be caught up by Christ in the atmosphere between earth and heaven. (It will be a visible snatching away of the ready believers.) We will be taken by Christ to the Father's home to be united with loved ones from ages past who have died and freed from all sin, sickness, disease, and death. We will have continual, uninterrupted Holy Communion with the Triune God. **"Then the saying that is written will come true: 'death has been swallowed up in victory.' 'Where, O death is your victory? Where, O death, is your sting?' The sting of death is sin, and the power of sin is the law. But thanks be to God! He gives us the victory through our Lord Jesus Christ"** (1 Corinthians 15:54b-57 NIV). We will no longer cry out for the glory but will be forever in the glory.

There are various views concerning the rapture of the church.

1) **The Pre-Tribulation Rapture**—Some scholars believe that the church will be raptured before the great tribulation period.

2) **Mid-Tribulation Rapture**—This teaching suggests that Jesus will rapture His church in the middle of the tribulation period.

3) **Post-Tribulation Rapture**—Christ will rapture his church at the end of the great tribulation period.

Neither the time nor the views concerning the rapture are as important to us as the truth that it will take place. To a "set apart" people who understand the words of Jesus, these views are not the main focus but the awesome truth that He is coming again for His bride and we must be ready. "**However, no one knows the day or hour when these things will happen, not even the angels in heaven or the Son Himself. Only the Father knows. And since you don't know when that time will come, be on guard! Stay alert!**" (Mark 13:32-33 NLT).

One day we, the ready church of God, will be taken away by Jesus to escape the wrath that is to come. According to the Scriptures, that day is uncertain and will happen unexpectedly. Jesus said that not even He, the Son of Man, knew the time. But we are to stay watchful and alert; keep faith alive because it will happen just as it is written in Scriptures. "**In the twinkling of an eye!**"

The rapture of God's church is imminent; it will take place suddenly. The signs of the time are all around us. It will happen in the twinkling of an eye and we, the ready believers, the carriers of God's glory, will be out of this world. The warning is to be ready. "**And we are instructed to turn from godless living and sinful pleasures. We should live in this evil world with wisdom, righteousness, and devotion to God. While we look forward with hope to that wonderful day when the** glory of our great God and Savior, Jesus Christ, will be revealed" (Titus 2:12-13 NLT).

In Jesus' letters to the churches, He warned them to make and keep themselves ready. Only two of the churches, Philadelphia and Smyrna, were pronounced ready by Jesus. The other churches (except for Sardis, which was pronounced dead) had a level of glory but were not walking in the glory. Today's churches are a lot like the churches to whom Jesus' letters were addressed. Jesus is coming for a ready church, a church without spot or wrinkle. He is coming for a church that is manifesting His glory on the earth. His bride must make herself ready and like the churches in Philadelphia and Smyrna; we must keep ourselves ready. **"I will ask nothing more of you except that you hold tightly to what you have until I come. To all who are victorious, who obey me to the very end, to them I will give authority over all the nations"** (Revelation 2:24b-27a NLT). The King of Glory will one day step down in resplendent glory for His ecclesia—His glorified church, His willing and obedient children. He will take His bride away. What a day that will be! He will command those gates and doors that are locked to be open and will by force seize His bride. **"Open up, ancient gates! Open up, ancient doors, and let the King of Glory enter"** (Psalm 24:7 NLT).

There will be no earthly weights capable of holding back the bride of Christ, but they will let go at His command and He will take His bride, the glorified believers to be with Him forever and ever. **"After that we who are still alive and are left will be caught up together with them (resurrected believers) in the clouds to meet the Lord in the air. And so we will be with the Lord forever"** (1 Thessalonians. 4:17 NIV). **"Open up, ancient gates! Open up, ancient doors, and let the King of Glory enter. Who is this King of Glory? The Lord of Heaven's Armies—He is the King of glory"** (Psalm 24:9-10 NLT).

QUESTIONS FOR REVIEW

1. What is the teaching of most Bible scholars concerning Revelation 4:1?

2. What is the meaning of the word rapture?

3. Who are the ones that will be raptured by Christ?

4. Will there be more than one rapture?

5. What is the blessed hope of every believer?

6. What is the meaning of the word ecclesia?

7. Will the rapture be visible to all mankind? Give the reason for your answer.

8. What are some of the benefits that the rapture believers will experience?

9. What are the three main views on the rapture listed in this chapter?

10. What is the warning given to believers in Titus 2:12-13?

11. According to the Scriptures, when will Jesus return?

12. How are you prepared for the rapture?

CHAPTER FIVE

When That Trumpet Sounds

"For the Lord Himself will come down from heaven with a commanding shout, with the call of the archangel, and with the trumpet of God. And the dead in Christ shall rise first: then we which are alive and remain shall be caught up together with them in the clouds, to meet the Lord in the air: and so shall we ever be with the Lord. So comfort and encourage each other with these words" (1 Thessalonians 4:16-18 KJV).

Death is not a permanent factor. No one who dies will remain dead. The grave is not the final destiny of man. One hymn writer wrote, "Judgment is surely coming, coming to you and me. We will be judged that morning for all eternity. Some will go into heaven, others will be denied, will you be in that number standing outside? Standing outside the portal, standing outside denied. Known that with the demons ever you shall abide. Never to share the beauty awaiting the sanctified. O what an awful picture standing outside" (A. McClung, 1961, *Judgment Is Surely Coming*). The important question to be answered by all is this: "Will you be a part of the denied or heaven qualified?"

The Bible tells us that one day Jesus Himself will descend from heaven with a commanding shout, with the call of the archangel and with the trumpet call of God. And all the dead in Christ shall rise from their graves. When Jesus steps out in time to usher in eternity, there will be a great stirring in the graves of the saints. The commanding shout of Jesus will arouse the dead saints. They will hear the voice of the Savior and the call of the archangel and the trumpet of God, and the grave will no longer have the power to hold them down.

They will respond to that glorious call and will rise to meet Him in the air. All across this great universe, out there in space, buried in the deepest ocean—wherever the bodies of those who die in Christ lie— they will all hear the call of Christ and the trumpet of God. When that trumpet sounds, in the twinkling of an eye they will rise and be caught up by the power of God to meet Jesus in the air!

Immediately after the dead in Christ rise, the Christians who are still alive on the earth will rise.

No weights of earth will be able to hold them back. They too will respond to the call of God and be caught up to meet the Lord in the air and escorted to that place that God has prepared. They will be forever with the Lord. The saints will stand united in God's presence safe and secure. Their souls will look back and wonder how they got over, but—praise God—they made it!

When that trumpet sounds, God will turn our tragedies to triumphs, our poverty to riches, our pain to glory, and our defeat to victory. When that trumpet sounds, it will usher out the old and usher in the new. The Bible says, **"The body that was sown is perishable."** That body that went into the grave was perishable. It was limited by the laws of nature. The body got frail, sickly, and decayed. But when that trumpet sounds, it will be raised imperishable.

The Bible says, **"It is sown in dishonor."** It was a weak body that went into the grave. But when that trumpet sounds, it will be raised in honor and glory. It will be full of the life-giving spirit of Christ and will be raised in power! The Bible says, **"It is sown a natural (terrestrial) body."** But when that trumpet sounds, it will be raised a supernatural (celestial) body. That is why as believers we never give up. Though our bodies are dying, our spirits are being renewed every day! Eventually we will outgrow this terrestrial body and be clothed in our spiritual body for all eternity.

As believers, we have a body that has been reserved in heaven that is just like Christ's. It is full of heaven's life and there is no expiration date. These bodies are perfect without any form of disability. The heavenly body never grows old; it never ages but remains the same. Thanks be to God that these earthly bodies that continuously fail us are not able to live forever!

The Bible says, **"We shall not all sleep,"** for when that trumpet sounds we shall all be changed in a moment, in the twinkling of an eye. At the sound of the commanding shout of our Lord, the call of the archangel and the trumpet call of God, this corruptible body that is prone to failure shall be changed. The saints who have died will be raised with transformed bodies. And the bodies of the saints who are alive will be transformed so that they will never die. It will be out with the old and in with the new for all eternity. The Bible says, **"When this happens— when our perishable bodies have been transformed into heavenly bodies that will never die—then at last the Scriptures will come true: 'Death is swallowed up in victory. O death, where is thy sting? O grave, where is thy victory? For sin is the sting that results in death, and the law gives sin its power. But thanks be to God, which gives us the victory through our Lord Jesus Christ!'"** (Corinthians 15:54-56 NLT.

When that trumpet sounds, it will be the dead in Christ and those who are living in Christ that will rise. Don't just think you are ready; be certain that you are. God has made all the provision that is needed to secure your salvation. **"For our evil consciences have been sprinkled with Christ's blood to make us clean, and our bodies have been washed with pure water"** (Hebrews 10:22b NLT). We must also remember that it is a terrible thing to fall into the hands of the living God. What about you, reader? When that trumpet sounds, will you be ready?

CHAPTER SIX

Glimpses into Christ's Glory

Revelation 4

All through the book of Revelation, we are given glimpses into Christ's glory. In chapter 1, Jesus introduces Himself as the fullness of God's eternal glory—He who was and is and is to come. In chapters 2 and 3, He deals with things which are now (the present glory), and in chapters 4-22, Jesus deals with things which are and which are to come (the glory in heaven and the latter glory; the full knowledge of it governing the earth). **"For this is what the Lord of heaven's Armies says: In just a little while I will again shake the heavens and the earth, the oceans and the dry land. I will shake all the nations, and the treasures of all the nations will be brought to this Temple. I will fill this place with glory, says the Lord of heaven's armies. The future glory of this temple will be greater than its past glory, says the Lord of heaven's Armies. And in this place I will bring peace. I, the Lord of heaven's Armies, have spoken!"** (Haggai 2:6-9 NLT).

The Opened Door

"A door was opened in heaven" (Revelation 4:1a NLT). In chapter 4 of the book of Revelation, John saw a door opened in heaven. The open door suggested that John had an open invitation to heaven. Jesus spoke of doors earlier in His letter to the church at Philadelphia. **"And I have opened a door for you that no one can close"** (Revelation 3:8A NLT). And again in chapter 3, verse 20 in His letter to the church at Laodicea. **"Look, I stand at the door and knock. If you hear my voice and open the door, I will come in, and we will share a meal together as friends."** But this door was different. It was not a door on the earth; it was a door opened in heaven. John was about to take a glimpse into Christ's heavenly glory. He was about to experience the glory of heaven. This door that was standing open in heaven was the door of glorious revelation. John was about to see things that were and are to come, and he was about to be given inexpressible glimpses into the glory of Christ.

John was about to see things too glorious for the human mind to understand. He was about to see and experience another realm of God's glory, situations and events that were too great for mere human mind and eyes. **"Come up here, and I will show you what must happen. After this and instantly I was in the Spirit and I saw a throne in heaven and someone sitting on it"** (Revelation 4:1b-2 NLT). Can you imagine hearing the voice of God calling you upward? The Spirit of the Lord had complete control of John. The Holy Spirit (the Spirit of glory) was taking John deeper and deeper into God's glory.

As the command is given for him to come up higher, John is instantly consumed by the power of the Holy Spirit and is led through the open door into heavenly glory, worship, and knowledge. He is about to be shown the glory that was and is and is to come. In heaven, John becomes the eyes and ears for believers on earth. It was a quick exit for John. In less than the blinking of an eye, he was out of this world and standing in heaven. **"And instantly I was in the Spirit"** (Revelation 4:2). Instantly this suggests to us a spontaneous departure from earth to heaven. The second the command was given, John was in heaven. John's "without hesitation" departure from earth may symbolize the church's sudden exit. Once the trumpet sounds, all ready believers will be out of this world and into heaven in a moment, in the twinkling of an eye. **"It will** happen in a moment, in the blinking of an eye, when the last trumpet is blown" (1 Corinthians 15:52a).

John was in heaven on a special assignment; he was not in heaven to stay. His experience was similar to Paul's writing of being taken up into heaven. "I was caught up to the third heaven fourteen years ago. Whether I was in my body or out of my body, I don't know, only God knows" (2 Corinthians 12:2 NLT). God allowed John to see and experience the glorious wealth of heaven's worship before revealing to Him earth's impending judgment. The message of the latter glory filling the earth had to be brought to earth. There on the isle of Patmos, God delighted in John's worship and knew that He was usable. Imagine the strength of your worship opening another level of God's glory that has never been experienced before. This is what happened to John.

The Three Heavens

The Bible teaches that God created the heavens. "In the beginning God created the heavens and the earth" (Genesis 1:1 NLT). Jewish teachings from the Scriptures suggests to us that there are three heavens. The first heaven comprises of the clouds and the atmosphere surrounding the earth,; the temporary abode of Satan. He rules from the first heaven. When he was thrown down from the third heaven, he began his temporary reign in the first heaven. "Satan, who is the god of this world, has blinded the minds of those who don't believe. They are unable to see the glorious light of the Good News. They don't understand this message about the glory of Christ, who is the exact likeness of God" (2 Corinthians 4:4 NLT).

The second heaven is known as that of the stars or stellar heaven, which is also called the universe or outer space. It is where the sun, moon, and stars dwell. Man with all his wisdom and knowledge will never be able to comprehend the starry heavens. The psalmist stood in awe of the heavens as he proclaimed. "The heavens tells of the glory of God. The skies display His marvelous craftsmanship" (Psalm 19:1 NLT).

In verses 3, 4, and 6, he exclaimed, "**They speak without a sound or a word; their voice is silent in the skies; yet their message has gone out to all the earth, and their words to all the world. The sun rises at one end of the heavens and follows its course to the other end. Nothing can hide from its heat.**" Isaiah wrote, "**He spreads out the heavens like a curtain and makes His tent from them**" (Isaiah 40:22 NLT). What a glorious starry expanse created by the King of Glory! And it is fittingly so, for beyond the glorious expanse lies the third heaven: the heaven of heavens.

The third heaven is God's abode, which is also known as paradise. In 2 Corinthians 12:2, Paul speaks of being caught up into God's abode. "**I was caught up into the third heaven fourteen years ago.**" He goes on in verse 4 to say, "**But I do know that I was caught up into Paradise and heard things so astounding that they cannot be told.**" The third heaven is beyond space and stars. It is a region far beyond the reach of humankind. Scientists have described the third heaven as an open space that man is unable to penetrate.

The third heaven is off limits to us, being clothed in these terrestrial bodies. John's body had to be transformed as he visited heaven. Paul could not explain his being caught up into paradise. "**Whether my body was there or just my spirit, I don't know; only God knows**" (2 Corinthians 12:3 NLT). It is a city and a dwelling place for all believers. "**You have come to Mount Zion, to the city of the living God, the heavenly Jerusalem, and to thousands of angels in joyful assembly**" (Hebrews 12:22 NLT).

Only those who qualify for the celestial body are able to penetrate the third heaven and dwell in that eternal city. As Jesus hung on that old rugged cross between two thieves, He assured the repentant thief that he would be with Him in paradise. "**And Jesus replied, 'I assure you, today you will be with me in paradise'**" (Luke 23:42 NLT). The repentant thief qualified for the celestial body; that very day he made an appearance in paradise.

Jesus passed through the heavens when He returned to glory and took His seat at the right hand of the Father. **"It was not long after He said this that He was taken up into the sky while they were watching, and He disappeared into the cloud"** (Acts 1:9 NLT). That is why the heavens cannot hold up a believer's blessing. Jesus has gone through and bestowed upon His church the same divine power to go through the heavens. Satan cannot hold up your blessings. Jesus' ascension destroyed every stronghold of the Devil. Whatever may be confronting you, divine power is yours to go through the heavens and get your blessing.

The Things Which Are to Come

The things which are to come are what we will study for the remainder of this book. These things which are to come are all about the latter glory. Everything that is to come will bring to earth a greater level of God's glory. It is a culmination of God's power and glory covering the earth as the waters cover the sea. It will be about the kingdoms of this world becoming the kingdom of our God and His eternal reign being established. **"And the Lord will be King over all the earth. On that day there will be one Lord—His name alone will be worshipped"** (Zechariah 14:9 NLT).

Jesus allowed John to show us heaven before allowing us to see what it will be like on earth, because once we get a glimpse of heaven the future conditions of earth will not cause us fear. We will be at peace knowing that God is in absolute control. We will be at peace knowing that God has made provision for His church to escape the final war between good and evil (the period of the tribulation). During the reign of the antichrist, when earth is in its final war with heaven, we (the ready believers) will be at peace in heaven around the throne of God captivated by the ineffable glory of heaven giving pure praise and worship to our King . . . Amen!

The Throne of God

Let's go into heaven with John: **"And I saw a throne in heaven and someone sitting on it"**

(Revelation 4:2 NLT). The throne of God is the central object of heaven; it is mentioned eleven times in chapter 4. The presence of a throne represents glory, authority, sovereignty, and the absolute reign of God. The glory of God is visible on the earth as it flows from His throne into the life of His church. The throne of God is the place of authority and the center of God's leadership for the activities of heaven on the earth. It is good to know that God is in absolute control because the horrific events of earth can sometime overwhelm us and shake our faith. When we don't know what to do and it seem like there is no way through, it is comforting to know that God is in absolute control. There is never a time when He is not in control or is weakened in His reign as King; He never leaves His throne. The psalmist says He never slumbers or sleeps. His reign is complete and His control is eternal.

The throne seems to be a fixed point in relationship with everything else in heaven. John tells us who is on the throne, what stands before the throne, what is the center of and around the throne, and what is directed toward the throne. John does not describe the throne or the One seated on it; both are indescribable. What he tries to describe is the glory of the One seated on the throne. **"The One sitting on the throne was as brilliant as gemstones—like jasper and carnelian"** (Revelation 4:3a NLT). Matthew Henry concluded that the jasper represents the holiness of God and the carnelian represents the consuming fire of His judgment.[7] John could only use symbols of precious stones to describe to us the glory of the One seated on the throne. We can only begin to imagine from His writing the depth of what he may have seen.

---

[7]   Matthew Henry, *Matthew Henry Commentary, Volume 6* (United States of America: Hendrickson Publishers, Inc., 1991), p. 917.

The Rainbow

"And the glow of an emerald circled his throne like a rainbow" (Revelation 4:3b NLT). In his book *Revelation Illustrated*, Tim LaHaye noted that this was no ordinary rainbow but a perfectly circular one. The circular rainbow represented the eternal nature of God and the emerald, His great mercy.[8] He is the eternal God, from everlasting to everlasting the same. His great mercy is new every morning. In His greatness, He has prepared new mercy for every day of our lives. It doesn't matter how long you may live and what you may go through; He has prepared new mercy for all your days. What a preeminent God!

We are unable to see the fullness of the rainbow on earth, but every so often He reminds us of His faithfulness by opening heaven and giving us a glimpse of the rainbow. A glimpse of the rainbow is an awesome reminder that He is in absolute control. It is a reminder of God's promises to us that will never fail. He is the faithful and everlasting God, full of grace and mercy, who never changes. "'I am the Alpha and the Omega—the beginning and the end,' says the Lord God. 'I am the one who is (the Lord), who always was (the Ancient of Days), and who is still to come (the amen)—the Almighty One'" (Revelation 1:8 NLT). He is from everlasting to everlasting God. He is the Lord Jehovah, the Alpha and Omega that sits upon the throne forever and ever. In the times of trouble, we can be confident that our God reigns!

The Twenty-Four Elders

"Twenty-four thrones surrounded Him, and twenty-four elders sat on them. They were all clothed in white and had gold crowns on their heads" (Revelation 4:4 NLT). Who are these twenty-four elders? Matthew Henry believed that they are men, patriarchs of the Old Testament and New Testament, while others believe them to be

---

[8]   Tim LaHaye, *Revelation Illustrated and Made Plain* (Grand Rapids Michigan: Zondervan Publishing House, 1975) p. 79.

angels or elders of angels.[9] Their true identity will be reveal on that great rapturous day. Who they are is not important to our faith and the keeping of our faith.

The revelation was given for us to be blessed and strengthened to be overcomers who are ready for our quick exit from earth. John was experiencing the order of heaven, the beauty of holiness through these revelations. We are to be empowered by this heavenly revelation to defeat the Devil at every level! We must not waste the hour through aimless arguments concerning the things that will profit us little or nothing, but let us run on to perfect that which is still imperfect.

In Revelation 5:11-12, these twenty-four elders were included in the song of worship to the Lamb that was slain. John said, **"Then I looked again, and I heard the singing of thousands and millions of angels around the throne and the living beings and the elders. And they sang in a mighty chorus: 'The Lamb is worthy-the Lamb who was killed. He is worthy to receive power and riches and wisdom and strength and honor and glory and blessing.'"** The worship song that was being sung by them described the Lamb as the Paschal Lamb worthy to break the seals and open the scroll. The entire heavenly host was proclaiming the worthiness of the Lamb of glory to break the seal and open the scroll. Can you imagine the sound of worship as they hail Jesus as being the One that was worthy? John said that they sang in a mighty chorus declaring the Lamb as the worthy One.

"From the throne came flashes of lightning and the rumble of thunder" (Revelation 4:5a NLT). The lightning and thunder are significant of heavenly events. This may have been a prelude of what was about to happen on the earth. Imageries of thunder and lightning were used in the Old Testament to depict the excellence of God's power and glory. David wrote, **"The Lord thundered from heaven; the voice of the Most High resounded amid the hail and burning coals. He shot His**

---

9   Matthew Henry, *Matthew Henry Commentary Volume 6* (United States of America: Hendrickson Publishers, Inc., 1991), p. 917.

arrows and scattered His enemies; His lightning flashed, and they were greatly confused" (Psalm 18:13-15 NLT). In the book of Exodus, at Mount Sinai when the Israelites were about to be given the laws of God, there was lightning and thunder. **"On the morning of the third day, there was a powerful thunder and lightning storm, and a dense cloud came down upon the mountain"** (Exodus 19:16 NLT).

The Sevenfold Spirit of God

"In front of the throne were seven torches with burning flames. This is the sevenfold Spirit of God (Revelation 4:5b NLT). The sevenfold Spirit of God is the sevenfold ministry of the Holy Spirit that every believer should strive to have operational in their life: The Spirit of the Lord, The Spirit of wisdom, the Spirit of understanding, the Spirit of council, the Spirit of might, the Spirit of knowledge, and the fear of the Lord (Isaiah 11:2 NLT). These are the characteristics of God's glory that will cover this earth as the water covers the sea floor. The strength of God will be revealed through ministries that are operating through this anointing of the Holy Spirit.

The kingdom of God comprises of the sevenfold ministries of the Holy Spirit. A church that is going from glory to glory operates under this anointing. All of the church's labor, love, and service to God must be governed by the sevenfold ministries of the Holy Spirit. The flow of glory in our lives is dependent upon the flow of these ministries. The manifestation of these ministries will control our lives when we are baptized into God and there is nothing left of us that can be used for His glory. God longs for a church that is functioning under the strength of these ministries. (For more on the sevenfold ministries of the Holy Spirit, see chapter 1 of this book.)

"In front of the throne was a shiny sea of glass, sparkling like crystal" (Revelation 4:6a NLT). John saw the brilliance of God's glory in all its colors and he described it as a shiny sea of glass, sparkling like crystal. He tried his best to describe the brilliance of God's glory that he saw before the throne. Glass, especially crystal-clear glass, was a rare commodity in New Testament times. What John saw was pure glory—glory that was indefinable and of great magnificence. No one could accurately describe the glory of God even as it is manifested here on the earth.

"In the center and around the throne were four living beings, each covered with eyes front and back. The first of these living beings had the form of a lion; the second looked like an ox; the third had a human face; and the fourth had the form of an eagle with wings spread out as though in flight" (Revelation 4:6b-7 NLT). George Eldon Ladd, in his *A Commentary on the Revelation of John*, describes these four living beings as cherubim (the highest order of the angels). They guard the throne of God, declaring God's holiness, and are known to be the worship leaders of heaven. Others believe that the four living beings represent the attributes of God: His majesty, faithfulness, power, intelligence, and sovereignty.

Jesus Christ is the object of worship in heaven and should be the object of our worship on the earth. When John was caught up into heaven, he experienced heavenly worship. How awesome it must have been! John began to understand the uniting of our worship here on the earth with that of heaven. As our praise and worship leaves the earth and ascends into the heavenly realm, it connects with heaven's worship and creates an atmosphere of glory here on the earth. When the Psalmist wrote, **"Who shall ascend the hill of the Lord? Or who shall stand in His holy place?"** (Psalm 24:3 KJV), he was talking about worship. Worship of God will take you up the hill of the Lord and into His holy place where you will experience the glory and the power of worship as you bow, unable to stand in adoration of the King.

Heaven is filled with great joy, praise, and worship. When the church gets into the heavenly mode of worship, there will be great joy, praise, and worship. We will serve the Lord with gladness. The church will be elevated and will experience the effects of heavenly worship. We will be seated in heavenly places in Christ Jesus. The joy will be doubled, the praise will be doubled, the worship will be doubled, and the glory will be doubled. The presence of God will illuminate the atmosphere. And His shekinah glory will be seen in the sanctuary. He will come and sit in the midst of His church in His beauty and splendor. The church too will experience the power and strength of the open heavenly door. When the worship flows from the heart and not just from the lips, we become a part of the heavenly worship and we become transfixed by His glorious presence.

I believe that we are nearing a day and time when the church will overflow with pure worship. There will be no awareness of time because we will be caught up in the splendor of worship and heaven will govern the atmosphere. We will sit for days at end enraptured by the glory of it all. We will allow the heavenly praise and worship to lead out in worship. Oh the power and glory of worship in heaven!

All of creation will one day bow in worship of the Creator God! They will praise and honor Him as His glory is revealed. He will not only be seen as Creator but as Creator and Sustainer of everything, the omnipotent and omniscient God, King of Kings, and Lord of all. On that day, His great mercy, grace, and love for all mankind will be unmasked. There will be no devil to destroy and deceive God's creatures, nor will our worship be marred by that old serpent. We shall see Him as He is and worship Him in the splendor of His glory forever and ever!

"But the time is coming and is already here when true worshipers will worship the Father in spirit and in truth. The Father is looking for anyone who will worship Him that way. For God is spirit, so those who worship Him must worship in spirit and in truth" (John 4:23-24 NLT). The Father is looking for true worshippers, the diligent seekers of His glory presence, those who will push on the earth realm coming up strong against the kingdom of darkness until they have access to heaven. They are the believers who will strive to go beyond the flesh, behind the veil, face-to-face, consumed by God's glory and grace. Why struggle outside Him when you can be secure in Him?

When believers reach that place of intimacy beyond the veil, they have moved from their space into God's. They have gone beyond the flesh and are lost in His wonder, love, and glory. David said, "**The one thing I ask of the Lord—the thing I seek most—is to live in the house of the Lord all the days of my life, delighting in the Lord's perfections and meditating in His temple**" (Psalm 27:4 NLT). David was a true worshipper. His thirst for the presence of God was real. His greatest desire was to live in the presence of the Lord each and every day of his life. He wanted to move in with God and not God moving in with him. He wanted to live where God lives in the beauty of His holiness. He wanted to live a selfless life that his spirit would be glorified. Oh that there were worshippers with the same passion today! Take me, Holy Spirit, to where God is. Let my desire be to see more of Him and less of me.

"**Day after day and night after night they keep on saying, 'Holy, holy, holy is the Lord God Almighty—the One who always was, who is, and who is still to come'** (Revelation 4:8 NLT). There is no end to worship in heaven; it is the place of endless praise and worship. It's the place of pure worship. The cherubim worshipped continually. The Bible says they worshipped day and night. They never ceased to give Him glory, and verses 9-11 say, "**Whenever the living beings give glory and honor and thanks to the one sitting on the throne, the One who lives forever and ever, the twenty-four elders fall down and worship the One who lives forever and ever. And they lay their crowns before the throne and say, 'You are worthy, O Lord our God, to receive glory and honor and power. For you created everything, and it is for your pleasure that they exist and were created.'**" They worshipped around the throne offering up pure praises to God. They are the worship leaders of heaven that summon all of heaven to worship. John saw the glorified beings in worship. What glimpses into Christ glory were experienced by John!

We are nearing the end of time. This world is running out of time and into eternity. We as believers should clothe ourselves in praise and worship of the King, glorious praise and worship of the King. Let us serve Him with gladness and make His presence known. This earth is our dressing room. The volume and perfection of our praise and worship here on the earth will prepare us for worship in heaven. We need to allow our praise of God to take us into Him, beyond the flesh where we bow in worship. The twenty-four elders bowed in worship of the One who sat upon the throne. They forgot about their thrones and their crowns and fell down in worship. When you are in worship, you lay aside everything that represents you and clothe yourself with the presence of God. You are in His space where a connection with the heavenly worship is experienced and you lose yourself in His glorious presence.

Jesus will come one day to take His Ecclesia away; He will come to gather His precious jewels. As we, ready believers, open ourselves to God, His ever-increasing power and glory will flow through our spiritual veins, causing an overflow of His glory and power on the earth. The ready believers are the worshippers who refuse to give up despite great opposition. They are not easily discouraged and frustrated. In the midst of trouble and trials, they just keep on worshipping. They have a blessed hope that nothing is able to weaken. They know that one day all evil will be erased and this earth will once again be covered with the pure glory of God. This world will once again become the kingdoms of our God and of His Christ, and He shall reign forever and ever! Are you one of the ready believers?

QUESTIONS FOR REVIEW

1. In chapter 4, what was the door that John saw opened in heaven?

2. Why was the door opened?

3. How long was John in heaven?

4. Describe some of the things John saw in heaven.

5. The things which are to come, what are they all about?

6. Why did Jesus allow John to show us the things in heaven before showing us what was to come on the earth?

7. What does the presence of a throne in heaven represent?

8. How did John describe the glory of the One seated on the throne?

9. In the Old Testament, what do the imageries of thunder and lightning suggest to us?

10. How did John describe the brilliance of God's glory that he saw before the throne?

11. What is the flow of glory in our lives dependent upon?

12. What do the four living beings represent in verses 6-7?

13. What glimpses of heaven's glory were revealed to you in this chapter?

CHAPTER SEVEN

A Greater Unfolding of God's Power and Glory

Revelation 5

In the preceding chapters of the book of Revelation, there is a greater unfolding of God's glory on the earth. The glory of God begins to intensify on the earth. There is rapid glory as God's plan for the end of the world is revealed. Heaven's power was taking over the nations of the earth at a rapid speed. God's glory begins to cover earth, land, and sea. The earth's atmosphere is charged with the ever-increasing power and glory of God. God's Word is becoming more and more intensifying on the earth. In chapter 4, John's attention was centered on the throne of God, but in chapter 5 he talks about the scroll and the importance of it being opened.

The Scroll

John said that a scroll was in the right hand of the One seated on the throne. **"There was writing on the inside and the outside of the scroll, and it was sealed with seven seals"** (Revelation 5:1b NLT). In John's day, all books were scrolls of either papyrus or vellum. This scroll seemed to be different. In ancient times, scrolls were read horizontally from right to left. The scrolls' writings were in columns about three inches wide and were written on a substance like brown paper. When a scroll was read, it was fastened with strings and the strings were sealed with wax at the knots. Scrolls would be held in the left hand and unrolled with the right.

The scroll that John saw was held in the right hand of the One on the throne, and, unlike the usual scroll, there was writing on the inside and outside. The scroll held the key to unlock the rest of Revelation that would be given to the church. It had the future events of earth that were about to be revealed to John. It contained a full revelation of the final triumph of the King of Glory over evil and His reigning in glory over all the earth.

The scroll revealed the events of a period known as the tribulation, a time of wrath and great suffering that includes God's glory judgment upon the earth and freeing this world from the grip of Satan's power. This will be a time of heaven reclaiming the kingdoms of this world and clothing them once again in the glory of God. **"For the time will come when all the earth will be filled, as the waters fill the sea, with an awareness of the glory of the Lord"** (Habakkuk 2:14 NLT).

John knew that the seven-sealed scroll had to be opened for evil to be eradicated and the reign of God established on the earth. And that a worthy person had to be found to break the seals. **"Then I wept because no one could be found who was worthy to open the scroll and read it"** (Revelation 5:4 NLT). John wept because he thought that no one was worthy enough to break the seals and open the scroll. No angel, no heavenly being, and no redeemed man in heaven or earth were considered worthy enough to open the scroll. All of the seals have to be open before the contents of the scroll can be revealed.

John knew that if there was not one worthy enough to break the seals and open the book, Satan would remain in control of the earth. **"Satan,** the god of this evil world, has blinded the minds of those who don't believe, so they are unable to see the glorious light of the Good News that is shining upon them" (2 Corinthians 4:4 a NLT). He knew that unless there was one found worthy enough to break the seals and unfold the scroll, this earth would never again be brought back to its original form. There would be no end to sickness, pain, frustration, sickness, and disease. Evil would reign forever from shore to shore. The power of darkness would forever be present. There would be no end to the pain of evil in the world. This world would never again be consumed by the glory of God. The power and glory of the cross would have been for naught. John wept at the thought of the scroll not being opened and evil prevailing against good forever! The seven-sealed scroll had to be opened!

Then one of the elders told John not to weep. There was One who was found worthy to break the seals and unroll the scroll. "But one of the twenty-four elders said to me, 'Stop weeping! Look, the Lion of the tribe of Judah, the heir to David's throne, has won the victory. He is worthy to open the scroll and its seven seals'" (Revelation 5:5 NLT). Jesus Christ, the Lion of the tribe of Judah, the heir to David's throne, the Paschal Lamb, the Potentate of glory, my Redeemer and your Redeemer, was found worthy. Oh thank God for Jesus! Thank God for his saving power! Thank God for his bleeding power! Thank God for the One who is worthy enough to be seated at the Father's right hand in defense of the saints!

Jesus was found worthy to break the seals and opened the scroll for the reclaiming of the kingdoms of this world back to the glory. There was no one else in all of heaven and earth that was worthy to break the seals. Jesus proved Himself worthy in humble submission to God by living a life of perfect obedience to the will of the Father. "While Jesus was here on earth, He offered prayers and pleadings, with a loud cry and tears, to the One who could deliver Him out of death. And God heard His prayers because of His reverence for God. So even though Jesus was God's Son, He learned obedience from the things He suffered. In this way, God qualified Him as a perfect High Priest, and He became the Source of eternal salvation for all those who obey Him" (Hebrews 5:7-9 NLT). He who is the Author and Finisher of our faith was found worthy to finish His triumphant defeat of Satan for all times. *Ride on, King Jesus . . . Ride on to victory!*

With the opening of the scroll by the Lamb that was slain from the foundation of the world, our *Perfect High Priest,* the period known as the tribulation began on the earth. And as each seal was broken, more and more of God's plan for end-time judgment, and the reestablishment of His glorious kingdom on the earth, was revealed. And with each revelation there was a great display of heaven's power and glory against evil!

John was in awe of what was being revealed. The intensity of what was disclosed was indescribable. It revealed the contents of the victorious battle between Christ the Lion, the King of Glory, and evil. It revealed the triumphant victory over all the forces of darkness, the antichrist, the battle of Armageddon, the beast and the false prophet, and the ultimate defeat of Satan. It revealed the expulsion of evil from the earth; it revealed the final judgment and the peace of the New Jerusalem. "**And Jerusalem will be filled, safe at last, never again to be cursed and destroyed**" (Zechariah 14:11 NLT). The scroll revealed the fulfillment of the blessed hope of all believers, the establishment of God's kingdom on the earth, and the eternal reign of heaven on the earth. "**And the Lord will be King over all the earth. On that day there will be one Lord—His name alone will be worshipped**" (Zechariah 14:9 NLT).

Jesus is the Defender of our faith and the Lord of the armies of heaven. He alone was found worthy to open the scroll. Someone once wrote, "Christ the Lion is victorious because of what Christ the Lamb has already done." Jesus was worthy to open the scroll because of His finished work on the cross of Calvary. The battle was fought and won at Calvary. The Lamb of glory now reigns as the King of Glory, the Lion of the tribe of Judah, because of the great exchange at Calvary. And His glorious kingdom is about to be established on the earth forever and ever! He is God of the 'turnaround.' He came in human form to undo what the Devil had done and accomplished the mission at Calvary . . . Alleluia! **"Then said I, 'Lo, I come (in the volume of the book it is written of me,) to do thy will, O God'"** (Hebrews 10:7 KJV). Now for the culmination of this great victory! Oh Alleluia, what a Savior!

Lamb of Glory

Although the angel refers to Jesus as the Lion of the Tribe of Judah, depicting His authority, power, might, and glory, John saw Him as the sacrificial Lamb. He saw Him as the Lamb of glory. He was seeing Him through the eyes of a blood-bought believer, a redeemed one who had accepted His great gift of salvation. He saw Him as the Paschal Lamb having been slain for the sins of man. He saw Him as the King of Glory having set captivity free. **"You were dead because of your sins and because your sinful nature was not yet cut away. Then God made you alive with Christ. He forgave all our sins. He canceled the record that contained the charges against us. He took it and destroyed it by nailing it to Christ's cross. In this way, God disarmed the evil rulers and authorities. He shamed them publicly by His victory over them on the cross of Jesus"** (Colossians 2:13-15 NLT).

Jesus' worthiness did not come from His eternal deity but from His being the sacrificial Lamb, the One that was slain, whose blood ransomed people for God. Those who reject so great a gift of salvation will see Jesus when He comes as the Lion (Judge of the earth), but those who believe and accept His free gift of salvation will receive Him as their Paschal Lamb, the King of Glory and the Lord of Lords.

The Opening of the Scroll

"And as He took the scroll, the four living beings and the twenty-for elders fell down before the Lamb. Each one had a harp, and they held gold bowls filled with incense—the prayers of God's people!" (Revelation 5:8 NLT). The Lamb, Jesus Christ, was found worthy to open the scroll that contained the events of the war between good and evil. There was no one else worthy enough to approach the throne and take the scroll from the right hand of God. All of heaven worshipped as the scroll was taken by the Lamb. The four living beings and the twenty-four elders sang a new song. **"You are worthy to take the scroll and break its seals and open it. For you were killed, and your blood has ransomed people for God from every tribe and language and people and nation. And you have caused them to become God's kingdom and His priests. And they will reign on the earth"** (Revelation 5:9 NLT). The finish work of Jesus was praised in this new song.

In verses 13 and 14 of chapter 5, John said, **"And then I heard every creature in heaven and on earth and under the earth and in the sea. They also sang: 'Blessing and honor and glory and power belong to the one sitting on the throne and to the Lamb forever and ever.' And the four living beings said, 'Amen!' And the twenty-four elders fell down and worshipped God and the Lamb."** Alleluia!

When Jesus took the scroll from the hand of the One seated on the throne, all of creation sang a song of worship. All of creation acknowledged Him as Lord. All of creation proclaimed His glory and worthiness! All of heaven rejoiced when the Lamb prevailed and the seal was broken and the scroll was opened. The twenty-four elders and the living creatures fell down in worship. The angelic beings fell down in worship. Every creature in heaven and earth and under the earth and in the sea began to worship. They all proclaimed Jesus worthy to receive power and riches, wisdom and strength and honor and glory and blessing . . . Amen!

Jesus alone is worthy to take the scroll from the hand of the One who sits on the throne and to reveal the future events of history for this earth. He holds the future and is in control of everything. Heaven sang a new song. **"And they sang a new song with these words: 'You are worthy to take the scroll and break its seals and open it. For you were killed, and your blood has ransomed people for God from every tribe and language and people and nation'"** (Revelation 5:9 NLT).

In the garden of Eden, Satan tried to rob God of His glory. He tried to discredit the created Word of God. Through Adam, He tried to dethrone God and spoil creation's plan. But he was defeated by the Lamb of glory, Jesus the Christ. God had given to Adam the title deed to this earth, and when Satan robbed him, he robbed mankind of their inheritance. That is why he is known as the god of this age.

But on the cross, Jesus destroyed his plans by crushing his head and stripping him of all his powers, by taking away the keys of death: hell and the grave. Satan's reign, his control, will end in ultimate defeat as the Lamb of glory takes back the title deeds. He, the Lamb of glory, will lead the battle as the King of Glory, the Lion of the tribe of Judah. Satan will be gloriously defeated for all times. **"Then the devil, who betrayed them, was thrown into the lake of fire that burns with sulfur, joining the beast and the false prophet. There they will be tormented day and night forever and ever"** (Revelation 20:10 NLT).

QUESTIONS FOR REVIEW

1. Describe the scroll John saw in the right hand of the One seated on the throne.

2. What was so unusual about this scroll compared to the scroll of that time?

3. What was on the scroll and why was it important for one to be found worthy to open it?

4. Why did John weep?

5. Who was found worthy to open the scroll and why?

6. What happened in the garden of Eden?

7. What happened as the Lamb took the scroll from the One seated on the throne?

8. Why is Satan known as the god of this age (2 Corinthians 4:4)?

9. What was the response of all creation when Jesus took the scroll out of the Father's hand?

10. What did Satan try to do in the garden of Eden?

11. How did Jesus destroy the plans of Satan?

CHAPTER EIGHT

The Cosmic Conflict between God and Satan: Part One

Revelation s 6-7

The tribulation period, the battle between good and evil, will be the darkest time this world has ever known. The church age will be over and it will be a very dark time for the believers who are left behind. It will be the worst time in the history of mankind. The *shekinah* glory of God, that visible perception that carried the church during the season of grace and was experienced by the raptured church, will not be readily accessible by those left behind.

In *The Encyclopedia Judaica, shekinah* is defined as "the divine presence, the numinous immanence of God in the world." The shekinah glory then is that glorious resting, abiding presence that carries the believers victoriously through their trials and disappointment. The Spirit of God is the numinous immanence of God in the world. The church age will be over; it will be a very dark and trying time for the believers in Christ who are left behind. It will be far worse than anything we are able to experience at present.

During the reign of the antichrist, the tribulation believers will be sorely tried and tested; some will even renounce their faith. It will be a time of great suffering, excruciating pain, and anguish on the earth. It will be seven years of indefinable terror that will touch all mankind. God never intended for His church to be a part of this period but that we will all be in heaven. Daniel, writing about this time, prophesied, **"Then there will be a time of anguish greater than any since nations first came into existence"** (Daniel 12:1 NLT).

This period will be a time of intense conflict between righteousness and wickedness. It will be a time of rapid glory as this world is taken out of the hand of the evil one and restored to its original glorious state. The very appearance of evil will be eradicated from the earth, making room for the glory of God to reign forever and ever. The glory will intensify until this earth is fully covered with the splendor of it even as it was in the days of Eden. It will be a glorified earth filled with the numinous immanence (divine presence) of God. Jesus describes this intense conflict known as the tribulation period as a time of great distress unequaled from the beginning of the world until now, and never to be equaled again. **"For that will be a time of greater horror than anything the world has ever seen or will ever see again"** (Matthew 24:21 NLT).

The rejection of Jesus as Lord and Savior by the world will bring about the period known as the tribulation. This time of intense judgment by God will be upon all those who rejected His Son Jesus Christ. It is the ultimate final victory over evil. Satan, the god of this age, will be dethroned and cast into the lake of fire never again to reign. **"Then the devil, who had deceived them, was thrown into the fiery lake of burning sulfur, joining the beast and the false prophet there they will be tormented day and night forever and ever"** (Revelation 20:10 NLT). He and all his angels will be thrown into hell along with all those who rejected Jesus as Lord and Savior.

This time of purging on the earth will start the very second after the church of God has been airlifted. As we are being airborne, the tribulation will be coming on down. We, the ready saints, will be carried away by the

King of Glory into the glory before the beginning of the tribulation story. Donald C. Stamps wrote, "The great tribulation will be the ultimate expression of accumulated evil in history and of God's judgments against an antichrist world, a specific period of terrible suffering and distress for people in all the world."[10] This earth will vibrate with the horrendous sound of suffering and pain as good triumphs over evil and the kingdoms of this world are taken out of the hand of the wicked one.

God's love is forever amazing. His great love for mankind is unending. Even in the midst of the tribulation, God's great judgment of earth, there will be great deliverance. Many scholars believe that the greatest revival ever to take place in Christendom will be during this time of pain and anguish. His unfailing love will still be reaching down toward man. What a merciful God! His glorious love will always be available to man. **"And I am convinced that nothing can ever separate us from God's love. Neither death nor life, neither angels nor demons, neither our fears for today or our worries about tomorrow—not even the powers of hell can separate us from God's love. No powers of hell can separate us from God's love. No power in the sky above or on the earth below—indeed, nothing in all creation will ever be able to separate us from the love of God that is revealed in Christ Jesus our Lord"** (Romans 8:38-39 NLT).

The hymn writer was right. "His love has no limits, His grace has no measure, His power no boundary known unto men; for out of His infinite riches in Jesus He giveth, and giveth, and giveth again" (Annie J. Flint, "He Giveth More Grace").

The persecution and suffering of the tribulation saints will be to the point of death. They will be imprisoned and tortured by the antichrist and his new world government. During this time of intense struggle, the antichrist will fight against the believers and defeat many of them. They will be beheaded, slain for the cause of Christ. Many who are

---

[10]   Donald C. Stamps, *Life in the Spirit Study Bible* (Grand Rapids, Michigan: Zondervan Corporation, 1985), p. 1475.

professing Christians now but who are not ready for the rapture will experience tribulation pain. The now cry from heaven to the believers is to escape this time of terror. It was never God's design for his children to go through this spiritual cosmic war. **"So stay awake and be prepared, because you do not know the day or hour of my return"** (Matthew 25:13 NLT).

The time of salvation is now. **"Today you must listen to His voice, don't harden your hearts against Him"** (Hebrews 4:7 NLT). You don't want to be left behind to face grave persecution, torture, and pain. The Lord has made a way of escape for every believer. We all can be rapture saints rather than tribulation saints. Let's accept His way of escape by staying ready for his return. **"So stay awake and be prepared, because you do not know the day or hour of my return"** (Matthew 25:13 NLT). Don't allow the work of the flesh to pull you out of that prepared zone. Stay alert and prepared, ready for His imminent return. **"So use your whole body as an instrument to do what is right for the glory of God. Sin is no longer your master, for you no longer live under the requirements of the law. Instead, you live under the freedom of God's grace"** (Romans 6:13b-14 NLT).

As we gaze into this cosmic conflict between God and Satan, there are three judgments that make up the tribulation period. The first is known as *the Seal judgments*—Revelation chapters 6-8. The second is known as *the Trumpet judgments*—chapters 8-11. And the final is known as *the Bowls (vials) judgments*—chapters 16-18. All of these judgments bring about a greater display and reign of God's power and glory on the earth. It's the deposing of Satan and the establishment of the eternal reign of Jesus as King of Kings and Lord of Lords. **"The God of heaven will set up a kingdom that will never be destroyed or conquered"** (Daniel 2:44b NIV).

Examining these judgments will help you to realize the horror that will be awaiting those who are left behind and hopefully create an evangelistic fever among us as believers to win the lost at any cost and to be watchful and ready, waiting for the glorious return of Christ. **"Be** dressed for service and well prepared, as though you were waiting for your master to return from the wedding feast. Then you will be ready to open the door and let him in the moment he arrives and knocks. There will be special favor for those who are ready and waiting for His return. I tell you, He Himself will seat them, put on an apron, and serve them as they sit and eat! He may come in the middle of the night or just before dawn. But whenever He comes, there will be special favor for His servants who are ready!" (Luke 12:35-38 NLT).

Seven-Seal Judgments

The breaking of the seals by Jesus will set in motion the final events of world history, the conclusion of the old world order and the radical establishment of the new. There will be wars and rumors of wars, famines, worldwide hunger, pestilences, and earthquakes in remote places. There will be massive bloodshed on the earth, lawlessness, and a great falling away from the faith. The breaking of each seal unleashed a greater level of God's judgment on the earth. "Then He added, 'Nation will go to war against nation, and kingdom against kingdom. There will be great earthquakes, and there will be famines and plagues in many lands, and there will be terrifying things and great miraculous signs from heaven'" (Luke 21:10-11 NLT).

The First Seal

"As I watched, the Lamb broke the first of the seven seals on the scroll. Then one of the four living beings called out with a voice that sounded like thunder, 'Come!' I looked up and saw a white horse. Its rider carried a bow, and a crown was placed on his head. He rode out to win many battles and gain the victory" (Revelation 6:1-2 NLT). The breaking of the first seal will release a spirit of false peace and the introduction of the antichrist; the man of lawlessness is revealed. A false sense of security will blanket the world only to be interrupted by the breaking of the next two seals that will release more intense judgments.

The Second Seal

"When the Lamb broke the second seal, I heard the second living being say, 'Come!' Then another horse appeared a red one. Its rider was given a mighty sword and the authority to take peace from the earth. And there was war and slaughter everywhere" (Revelation 6:3 NLT). There will be immeasurable suffering and anguish, bloodshed and death, with the breaking of the second seal. The false peace that would have blanketed the earth will suddenly come to an end. There will be a time of warfare upon the earth unlike any other time.

The Third Seal

"When the Lamb broke the third seal, I heard the second living being say, 'Come!' I looked up and saw a black horse, and its rider was holding a pair of scales in his hand. And I heard a voice from among the four living beings say, 'A loaf of wheat bread or three loaves of barley will cost a day's pay. And don't waste the olive and wine'" (Revelation 6:5-6 NLT). This famine will be unlike anything the world has ever experienced. There will be scarcity of food upon the earth, creating worldwide hunger and excruciating pain in every nation of the earth. Man will find it extremely difficult to survive.

The Fourth Seal

With the breaking of the fourth seal judgment, the spirit of death will intensify on the earth and claim the bodies of one-fourth of the world's population. "And I looked, and behold a pale horse: and his name that sat on him was Death, and Hell followed with him. And power was given unto them over the fourth part of the earth, to kill with sword, and with hunger, and with death, and with the beasts of the earth" (Revelation 6:8 KJV). Death and Hell devoured one-fourth of the world's population in this single judgment. "**But all this is only the beginning of the horrors to come**" (Matthew 24:8 NLT).

The Fifth Seal

"**And when the Lamb broke the fifth seal, I saw under the altar the souls of all who had been martyred for the word of God and for being faithful in their witness. They called loudly to the Lord and said, 'O Sovereign Lord, holy and true, how long will it be before you judge the people who belong to this world for what they have done to us? When will you avenge our blood against these people?'**" (Revelation 9-10 NLT). The breaking of the fifth seal revealed the souls of all those who had been slain for the sake of the gospel. John saw the souls of the martyred saints. It was a very moving sight. These martyred saints were crying out for God to defend their persecutors: those who denied them a place on the earth as the voice of God and those who were responsible for their merciless death.

John heard the loud cry of the martyred saints and then he noticed the tender response that was made to this cry. They were given white robes and told to rest a little longer. They were not actual robes that were given. Matthew Henry believes that the white robes are the robes of victory and honor. The martyred saints had not yet been resurrected. But these robes represent all the glory that will be the believers' experience in heaven. They speak for God's entire gift of righteousness, honor, and blessedness for the faithful saints.

They were told to rest a little longer. "**Then a white robe was given to each of them. And they were told to rest a little longer until the full number of their brothers and sisters—their fellow servants of Jesus—had been martyred**" (Revelation 6:11 NLT). John saw these martyred saints resting at the feet of Jesus. Man can only kill the body of a believer, and after physical death the soul enjoys life in the presence of the Father. What sweet repose was being experienced by these martyred saints! God has provided a better place for those who remain faithful to death.

Martyred saints have a reserved place of honor in heaven. These glorified saints were told to rest, for many more will die for their faith. It is difficult for these martyred saints to understand why their persecutors were still alive, yet God asks them to trust Him. There are times when you wonder about the prosperity of the wicked and when justice will be served. We are encouraged through the Word to rest, to wait on God; don't worry about the wicked. **"Fret not thyself because of evildoers"** (Psalm 37:1a KJV). It's a temporal prosperity. They will not last forever. God has a set time against the wicked. **"Rest in the Lord, and wait patiently for Him"** (Psalm 37:7a KJV). God will always be in absolute control. There will never be a time when He loses control . . . Rest!

The Sixth Seal

The cosmic conflict between God and Satan continued as the Lamb broke the sixth seal. With the opening of the sixth seal, there were great calamities on the earth. Great fear came upon the world as this earth began to tremble and shake under the powers of heaven and the glory of the Lord began to cover it.

The calamitous judgment of God that is revealed through the breaking of the sixth seal is horrific. **"I watched as the lamb broke the sixth seal, and there was a great earthquake. The sun became as dark as black cloth, and the moon became as red as blood. Then the stars of the sky fell to the earth like green figs falling from trees shaken by mighty winds. And the sky was rolled up like a scroll and taken away. And, all of the mountains and all of the islands disappeared. Then the kings of the earth, the rulers, the generals, the wealthy people, the people with great power, and every slave and every free person—all hid themselves in the caves and among the rocks of the mountains. And they cried to the mountains and the rocks, 'Fall on us and hide** us from the face of the One who sits on the throne and from the wrath of the Lamb. For the great day of their wrath has come, and who will survive?'" (Revelation 6:12-17 NLT).

The happenings of this sixth seal judgment will be so destructive and frightful that men everywhere will know that God and God alone is responsible. It will be a cosmic catastrophe that is incomparable to any other. The inhabitants of earth, including kings, generals, and all world rulers, will run and try to hide from the wrath of God, but there will be no place of security on the earth. There will be no person great or small who will escape the wrath of the Almighty God. Jesus spoke of this time in the Olivet Discourse. **"Immediately after the tribulation of those days shall the sun be darkened, and the moon shall not give her light, and the stars shall fall from heaven, and the powers of the heavens shall be shaken"** (Matthew 24:29 KJV).

As the inhabitants of earth see God sitting on the throne, they will experience intense fear and will cry out for the mountains and the rocks to cover them. No ungodly people will survive this day of the Lord! They will be totally exposed to His wrath. There will be no place to hide. The only survivors will be those who kept the faith in the midst of persecution. **"And they cried to the mountains and the rocks, 'Fall on us from the face of the One who sits on the throne and from the wrath of the Lamb. For the great day of their wrath has come, and who will be able to survive?'"** (Revelation 6:16, 17 NLT).

The seventh seal could not be opened until the seal of God was placed on the faithful tribulation saints foreheads. **"Then I saw four angels standing at the four corners of the earth, holding back the four winds from blowing upon the earth. Not a leaf rustled in the trees, and the sea became as smooth as glass. And I saw another angel coming from the east, carrying the seal of the living God. And he shouted out to those four angels who had been given power to injure land and sea, 'Wait! Don't hurt the land or the sea or the trees until we have placed the seal of God on the foreheads of His servants'"** (Revelation 7:1-3 NLT).

During this time of great cosmic upheaval, God will preserve the faithful tribulation saints. He will preserve them from this hour of perilous judgment upon the world. His seal will be placed upon their foreheads. Nothing will be able to harm or destroy them. They will be forever safe from the wrath of God. They will go through the hour of judgment, but the seal of God will shield them. The faithful believers are always safe from the fiery darts of the enemy. They never have to worry about the evil weapons that may be formed against them. God is their fortress protecting them from all danger. He will always take care of the godly. **"Day by day the Lord takes care of the innocent, and they will receive an inheritance that lasts forever. They will not be disgraced in hard times; even in famine they will have more than enough"** (Psalm 37:18-19 NLT).

The seal of God was to preserve the believers from the time of cosmic horror that was about to flood the earth. Although on the earth the believers were not going to experience the judgments of God against the ungodly, they were being given supernatural strength and courage to make it through this time of severe persecution. They will be a part of the triumphant overcomers.

The angels who were given the power to injure land and sea were told to wait until the servants of God were marked with the seal of God on their foreheads. God is always protective of His children. He has our names written in the palm of His hand. He will never allow the judgment of the unrighteous to destroy the righteous. The Lord knows those who are His and He will be their Shield and Defender in the times of trouble. **"The Lord hears His people when they call to Him for help. He rescues them from all their troubles . . . The righteous face many troubles, but the Lord rescues them from each and every one. For the Lord protects them from harm—not one of their bones will be broken!"** (Psalm 34:17; 19-20 NLT).

Although many of the sealed believers will go through great trials and persecution, even to the point of death, they will be protected from spiritual harm. Their destiny is secure and no man (not even the antichrist) will be able to break their faith in God. The seal of God (the glory of God) will be their covering in the midst of the cosmic conflict. What love is shown to the tribulation saints by God! "**The Lord Almighty says, 'The day of judgment is coming, burning like a furnace. The arrogant and the wicked will be burned up like straw on that day. They will be consumed like a tree—roots and all. But for you who fear my name, the Sun of Righteousness will rise with healing in His wings. And you will go free, leaping with joy like calves let out to pasture. On the day when I act, you will tread upon the wicked as if they were dust under your feet,' says the Lord Almighty**" (Malachi 4:1-3 NLT).

"**And I heard how many were marked with the seal of God. These were 144,000 who were sealed from all the tribes of Israel: There were 12,000 from each of the tribe. After this I saw a vast crowd (multitude) too great to count, from every tribe and people and language, standing in front of the throne and before the Lamb**" (Revelation 7:4-9a; paraphrasing mine). Scholars believe that the number 144,000 is 12 x 12 x 1,000, which symbolizes completeness—all God's children will be safe from the time of great judgments. Not one of God's faithful tribulation saints will be overlooked![11]

In verse 9, John saw a great multitude that was impossible to count standing before the throne. "**They were clothed in white and held palm branches in their hands. And they were shouting with a mighty shout, 'Salvation comes from our God on the throne and from the Lamb!' And all the angels were standing around the throne and around the elders and the four living beings. And they fell face down before the throne and worshipped God. They said, 'Amen! Blessing and glory and wisdom and thanksgiving and honor and power and strength belong to our God forever and ever. Amen!'**" (Revelation 7:9b-12 NLT). They were all engaged in high worship before the throne of God. The glory around them was so dazzling and the presence of

---

[11]   *Life Application Study Bible* (Carol Stream, Illinois: Tyndale House Publishers, Inc., 1988), p. 2050.

God so illuminating that they fell face down before His throne. What glorious rapture to be engaged in worship before the throne of God!

"Then one of the twenty-four elders asked me, 'Who are these who are clothed in white? Where did they come from?' And I said to him, 'Sir, you are the one who knows.' Then he said to me, 'These are the ones who died in the great tribulation. They have washed their robes in the blood of the Lamb and made them white'" (Revelation 7:13-14 NLT). John saw the glorious scene of heavenly worship by the great multitude of saints and was asked by one of the elders of their identity. Why would one of the twenty-four elders ask John the identity of the multitude? John told the elder that he (the elder) would know the answer. The elder then revealed the identity of the worshippers as those who came out of the great tribulation and did not give up, but against great odds they persevered.

Can you imagine your spiritual survival of the dreadful tribulation period? These saints were in high praise because they were overcomers of the most horrific time of evil on the earth. They survived! They were faithful to Christ even in the midst of great persecution and death, and now they were experiencing the joys of glory! They were rejoicing because now they were safe in heaven. They pushed through and overcame and now they were standing before the throne of God in high praise. They were seen enjoying the blessings of heaven after enduring the evil of earth. Their glorious faith had become sight and had brought them face to face with their heavenly King in glory.

Some of them would have died and others would have been martyred during the tribulation; they went through that horrendous time without giving up on their faith. Now here they stood in the midst of glory, giving to God the glory. "That is why they stand in front of God's throne and serve Him day and night in His temple. And He who sits on the throne will give them shelter. They will never again be hungry or thirsty; they will never be scorched by the heat of the sun. For the Lamb on the throne will be their shepherd. He will lead them

to springs of living water. And God will wipe every tear from their eyes" (Revelation 7:15-17 NLT).

God Himself, not one of the heavenly beings, will wipe every tear from their eyes . . . Alleluia! The horrific events of the tribulation period will never again be remembered by these saints. God will remove from their memory all that may have caused them suffering, regret, or remorse. The hymn writer was right. "It will be worth it all; when we see Jesus, Life's trials will seem so small when we see Christ, one glimpse on his dear face all sorrow will erase, so bravely run the race till we see Christ," (Esther Kerr Rusthoi, 1941, "When We See Christ"). These horrific activities will increase on the earth until sin is no more and the splendor of God is covering the earth. What glory!

QUESTIONS FOR REVIEW

1. Define the shekinah glory of God.

2. The tribulation period will be _____
   this world has ever known.

3. In one to two paragraphs, describe the tribulation period.

4. What will bring about the period known as the tribulation?

5. How many judgments make up the tribulation period?

6. Give a brief narrative of the occurrences on the earth during the
   breaking of the first four seals.

7. What did the breaking of the fifth seal reveal in heaven?

8. What did the breaking of the sixth seal reveal? Describe it.

9. How will God preserve His faithful saints during this time of
   judgment?

10. In a paragraph or two, write why it is worth your going through
    earthly trials and disappointments.

CHAPTER NINE

The Cosmic Conflict between God and Satan: Part Two

(Revelation 8-12)

<u>The Seventh Seal—The Trumpet Judgments</u>

"When the Lamb broke the seventh seal on the scroll, there was silence throughout heaven for about half an hour. I saw the seven angels who stand before God, and they were given seven trumpets" (Revelation 8:1-2 NLT). The opening of the seventh seal reveals the seven-trumpet judgment. The Bible says that there was silence throughout heaven for about half an hour. Can you imagine absolute silence throughout heaven? There were no sounds of praise and worship coming from the heavenly beings; nor were there any sounds coming from the throne of God. It was a holy hush as all of heaven stood silent in the presence of the Lord, knowing they were about to witness the frightful, dreaded events of the trumpet judgments that were about to be released upon the earth and upon the heavens. **"Stand in silence in the presence of the Sovereign Lord, for the awesome day of the Lord's judgment has come"** (Zephaniah 1:7 NLT).

Prayers of the Saints

"Then another angel with a gold incense burner came and stood at the altar. And a great amount of incense was given to him to mix with the prayers of God's people as an offering on the gold altar before the throne. The smoke of the incense, mixed with the prayers of God's holy people, ascended up to God from the altar where the angel had poured them out. Then the angel filled the incense burner with fire from the altar and threw it down upon the earth; and thunder crashed, lightning flashed, and there was a terrible earthquake" (Revelation 8:3-5 NLT). What a comforting passage of Scripture for the praying believer! Our prayers are never wasted but stored up in heaven until God's appointed time! The prayers of all God's people—the tribulation saints on the earth and the saints in heaven—are treasured by God. The smoke from the incensed prayers ascended into the nostril of God, and He responded as only God can.

All of heaven watched as God responded to the prayers of His children. God answers prayer and will never neglect any of His children's cries. The angel took the incense burner and filled it with fire from the altar. Then he threw the incense burner down upon the earth, causing strange disturbances, such as crashing thunder, lightning, and earthquakes. But this was just the prelude to the seven terrible trumpet judgments that were about to be revealed.

The Seven Trumpet Judgments

The seven trumpet judgments seem to be in response to the believers prayers. As the prayers of the faithful ascended before God, a third of creation was about to be judged. The angel took the censer with the incensed prayers and threw it to the earth and a token judgment followed: thunder crashed, lightning flashed, and there was a terrible earthquake. The stage was now set for God to avenge His people from the evil of the godless, calling the forces of good and evil to battle.

What will follow this heavenly firework is beyond words as the first four trumpets are blown.

The First Trumpet

"Then the seven angels with the seven trumpets prepared to blow their mighty blasts. The first angel blew his trumpet, and hail and fire mixed with blood were thrown down on the earth. One-third of the earth was set on fire, one-third of the trees were burned, and all the green grass was burned" (Revelation 8:6-7 NLT). As the first angel blew the trumpet, a warning, a heed to repentance, was issued. But was anyone really listening? One-third of earth population was destroyed by hail and fire mixed with blood. One-third of the trees and all the green grass were burned. What horror for those who will be left behind to endure the wrath of God's judgment!

The Second Trumpet

"Then the second angel blew his trumpet, and a great mountain of fire was thrown into the sea. One-third of the water in the sea became blood, one-third of all things living in the sea died, and one-third of all the ships on the sea were destroyed" (Revelation 8:8, 9 NLT). With the blowing of the second trumpet, there was increase judgment upon the earth. The Bible says a *great* mountain of fire was thrown into the sea and a third of the sea was judged. There was massive destruction on the seas. One-third of all living things in the sea and one-third of all ships on the sea were destroyed. But like the days of Pharaoh, man's heart was hardened toward God.

The Third Trumpet

"Then the third angel blew his trumpet, and a great star fell from the sky, burning like a torch. It fell on one-third of the rivers and on the springs of water. The name of the star was bitterness. It made one-third of the water bitter, and many people died from drinking the bitter water" (Revelation 8:10, 11 NLT). At the blowing of the third trumpet, the star that fell to earth polluted the rivers and springs of water, causing one-third of them to become bitter. Many people died from drinking this polluted water. However, there was still no desire in people to turn their hearts toward God.

The Fourth Trumpet

"Then the fourth angel blew his trumpet, and one-third of the sun was struck, and one-third of the moon, and one-third of the stars, and they became dark. And one-third of the day was dark, and also one-third of the night" (Revelation 8:12 NLT). The blast of this trumpet caused one-third of the luminaries to be darkened. A third of the sun, moon, and stars was struck by this fourth blast and the twenty-four-hour cycle of day and night was changed. But there was still greater terror to come.

"Then I looked, and I heard a single eagle crying, loudly as it flew through the air, 'Terror, terror, terror to all who belong to this world because of what will happen when the last three angels blow their trumpets'" (Revelation 8:13 NLT). After the blast and calamities of the fourth trumpet, an eagle is seen flying and heard crying over the earth warning the earth of the dreaded terror that is to come. It was a warning that the next three trumpet judgments would be much more intense and ruinous than those that preceded them.

The Fifth Trumpet

"Then the fifth angel blew his trumpet, and I saw a star that had fallen to earth from the sky, and he was given the key to the bottomless pit. When he opened it, smoke poured out as though from a huge furnace, and the sunlight and air turned dark from the smoke"

(Revelation 9:1-2 NLT). The blowing of the fifth trumpet brought about increased demonic activity. A star falls from heaven and is given the key to the bottomless pit. With the opening of the pit, smoke pours out and darkens the sun and air.

In verses 3-5, John sees locusts coming forth from the smoke. They were given the power to sting like scorpions. The activities of these locusts with scorpion-like power were limited by God. The Creator God is always in absolute control of His creation. There is never a time when He loses control. They were told not to harm the grass, plants, or trees but to torture those who did not have the seal of God on their foreheads. **"They were told not to harm the grass or plants or trees, but only the people who did not have the seal of God on their foreheads. They were told not to kill them but to torture them for five months with pain like the pain of a scorpion sting"** (Revelation 9:4-5 NLT). The sealed saints of God were sheltered from this time of torment.

"In those days people will seek death but will not find it. They will long to die, but death will flee from them!" (Revelation 9:6 NLT). What horror awaiting those who reject the saving power of Jesus Christ! During this time of torment, the unbelievers will try to commit suicide but will not succeed. During these five months, the spirit of death will have no display of power. The desire to die will not be granted. God and God alone will display His power and glory. All people who do not have the seal of God on their foreheads will go through this time of unmerciful torment. Can you imagine being stung by a scorpion and having to endure the effects of that sting for five months, your wanting to die and not being able too? **"The first terror is past, but look, two more terrors are coming!"** (Revelation 9:12 NLT).

The Sixth Trumpet

"Then the sixth angel blew his trumpet, and I heard a voice speaking from the four horns of the gold altar that stands in the presence of God. And the voice said to the sixth angel who held the trumpet,

'Release the four angels who are bound at the great Euphrates River.' Then the four angels who had been prepared for this hour and day and month and year were turned loose to kill one-third of all the people on earth" (Revelation 9:13-15 NLT). The sixth angel blew his trumpet and immediately John heard a voice from the four horns of the golden altar before God, giving the command to release the four angels who were bound at the great Euphrates. These four angels were probably fallen angels or demons, as they did not have the power to release themselves. They were limited in their destruction of mankind on the earth. God had set limits on the destruction. They only did what God allowed them to.

"I heard the size of their army, which was 200 million mounted troops. And in my vision, I saw the horses and the riders sitting on them. The riders wore armor that was fiery red and dark blue and yellow. The horses had head like lions, and fire and smoke and burning sulfur billowed from their mouths. One-third of all the people on earth were killed by these three plagues—by the fire and smoke and burning sulfur that came from the mouth of the horses. Their power was in their mouths and in their tails. For their tails had heads like snakes, with the power to injure people" (Revelation 9:16-19 NLT). This army was being led by the four angels that were released. It was an army of two hundred million horsemen. They bore the plagues of fire, smoke, and burning sulfur. A third of mankind was killed by these plagues. The power to kill lay in their mouths, and tails like serpent heads had the power to injure people.

"But the people who did not die in these plagues still refused to repent of their evil deeds and turn to God. They continued to worship demons and idols made of gold, silver, bronze, stone, and wood— idols that can never see nor hear nor walk! And they did not repent of their murders or their witchcraft or their sexual immorality or their thefts" (Revelation 9:20-21 NLT). The people's heart was hardened. They were consumed by Satan's power. They believed his lies and allowed the lies to control their very existence. Even after the plagues, they showed no fear of God. They continued in sin, worshipping demons and idols. They showed no fear of God's judgments. They continued with their godless ways of life. Their hearts were hardened toward their Maker. **"The human heart is the most deceitful of all things, and desperately wicked. Who really knows how bad it is?"** (Jeremiah 17:9 NLT).

There is an interlude between the sixth trumpet and the seventh trumpet with three visions that were designed to encourage the tribulation saints. In the first vision, John describes a mighty angel coming down from heaven surrounded by a cloud and with a rainbow over his head. He held a small scroll in his hands. He stood with his right foot on the sea and his left foot on the land, symbolizing that the message was for all of creation. His assignment was to announce the final judgments on the earth. **"Then I saw another mighty angel coming down from heaven, surrounded by a cloud, with a rainbow over his head. His face shone like the sun, and his feet were like pillars of fire. And in his hand was a small scroll that had been opened"** (Revelation 10:1-2a, NLT).

The mighty angel gave a shout like the roar of a lion. The seven thunders responded to his shout. John was forbidden to write the things which the thunders expressed. He heard a voice from heaven telling him to keep the things a secret. Although John was forbidden to reveal the message of the seven thunders, we can conclude that the seven peals of thunder suggest God's coming wrath and judgment.

The angel standing on the sea and land with his right hand raised toward heaven swore on oath that there would be no delay. **"When the seventh angel blows his trumpet. God's mysterious plan will be fulfilled. It will happen just as He announced it to His servants the prophets"** (Revelation 10:6b, 7 NLT). In the book of Ephesians, Paul wrote, **"God has now revealed to us His mysterious plan regarding Christ, a plan to fulfill His own good pleasure. And this is the plan: At the right time He will bring everything together under the authority of Christ— everything in heaven and on earth"** (Ephesians 1:9, 10 NLT). However there are truths concerning God that will not be revealed until His glory is established on the earth from sea to sea and shore to shore.

"Then the voice from heaven called to me again: 'Go and take the unrolled scroll from the angel who is standing on the sea and on the land.' So I approached him and asked him to give me the little scroll. 'Yes, take it and eat it,' he said. 'At first it will taste like honey, but when you swallow it, it will make your stomach sour!' So I took the little scroll from the hands of the angel, and I ate it! It was sweet in my mouth, but it made my stomach sour' (Revelation 10:9, 10 NLT). The scroll that John ate was sweet in His mouth because it was the truth of God. But the weight of judgment that was in the truth made his stomach sour. The prophet Ezekiel had a similar experience. "'Son of man, eat what I am giving you—eat this scroll!" So I opened my mouth, and he fed me the scroll. 'Eat it all,' he said. And when I ate it, it tasted as sweet as honey" (Ezekiel 3:1a-3 NLT).

Two Amazing Witnesses

"And I will give power to my two witnesses, and they will be clothed in burlap and will prophesy during those 1,260 days. These two prophets are the two olive trees and the two lamp stands that stand before the Lord of all the earth" (Revelation 11:3-4 NLT). Let's look at these amazing two witnesses. Who are they? Tim LaHaye says this about them: "Because God has not chosen to tell us exactly who they are, we can only offer a suggestion. Some of the most reliable suggestions are Elijah and Enoch; or Elijah and John the Baptist; or Elijah and Moses" [12] Their physical identity was not revealed by God. He chooses to identify them as "my two witnesses."

The popular belief is that these two amazing witnesses are Moses and Elijah. These were the two who ministered to Jesus on the mount of transfiguration. Moses, because he played a vital part in Israel's history, leading them out of Egypt and all through the wilderness. And Elijah, because in the history of Israel he is known as the greatest prophet. He

---

12   Tim LaHaye, *Revelation Illustrated and Made Plain* (Grand Rapids, Michigan: Zondervan Publishing House, 1975), p. 150.

was the one who shut and opened the heavens by the sound of his voice. John referred to them as the two olive trees and the two lampstands that stand before the Lord of all the earth. The *Life in the Spirit Study Bible Commentary* suggests that the olive trees represented the kingly and priestly ministries of Jesus. The lampstand symbolizes the church of Jesus Christ.[13] Their ministry will be empowered by the anointing of the Holy Spirit to display the power and glory of God on the earth. They will represent the true church on the earth.

"If anyone tries to harm them, fire flashes from their mouths and consumes their enemies. This is how anyone who tries to harm them must die. They have power to shut the sky so that no rain will fall for as long as they prophesy. And they have the power to turn the rivers and oceans into blood, and to strike the earth with every kind of plague as often as they wish" (Revelation 11:5-6 NLT). These two amazing witnesses will be given *dunamis* (dynamic) power, the power of God to operate on the earth. They will perform their ministry in the power of the Holy Spirit. They will be God's clear witnesses during the first half of the tribulation. No man, not even the antichrist, will be able to stand against these two witnesses until God allows him to. **"If anyone tries to harm them, fire flashes from their mouths and consumes their enemies"** (Revelation 11:5a NLT).

"When they complete their testimony, the beast that comes up out of the bottomless pit will declare war against them, and he will conquer them and kill them" (Revelation 11:7 NLT). The two witnesses will not die until their work is completed. The purpose of God in them will keep these two amazing witnesses alive. The beast (antichrist) will declare war against the two witnesses and kill them because of their prophetic words during the tribulation period. It is interesting to note that they cannot be killed until their mission is completed. They will be empowered to live, until God release them to die. They were clothed in the glory of God and covered until their course had been run.

---

13   Donald C. Stamps, *Life in the Spirit Study Bible* (Grand Rapids Michigan: Zondervan Corporation, 1985), p. 2056

Our faithful acts of obedience will keep us alive and well until our mission has been completed and God releases us to die, and even then death becomes only a stepping-stone into the glory. Nothing evil will be able to penetrate the glorious covering of God over the true believer's life. **"He will cover you with His feathers. He will shelter you with His wings. His faithful promises are your armor and protection"** (Psalm 91:4 NLT).

"And their bodies will lie in the main street of Jerusalem, the city that is figuratively called 'Sodom' and 'Egypt' the city where their Lord was crucified. And for three and a half days, all peoples, tribes, languages, and nations will stare at their bodies. No one will be allowed to bury them" (Revelation 11:7-9 NLT). Centuries ago, man would not be able to see how this would be possible, how all the earth would be able to gaze upon these two amazing witnesses bodies as they lie in front of the temple in Jerusalem. But today we know that everything has already been put in place to stare at these bodies from our homes and workplaces. These two bodies will be seen worldwide, wherever there is a television set that is in working condition. Even in death, the glory and power of God will be displayed through these two lifeless bodies lying in the main street of Jerusalem. No one will be allowed to bury them. When their voices will be silenced by the enemy, their bodies will still be used as a testimony of God's power and righteousness.

"All the people who belong to this world will gloat over them and give presents to each other to celebrate the death of the two prophets who had tormented them" (Revelation 11:10 NLT). The people of this world, those who have the mark of the beast, will rejoice over the death of these two amazing prophets. They will begin to feel secure in their sinful condition. There will be no fear of God among them. They will exchange gifts to each other in celebration of the death of these two amazing witnesses. This time of intense wickedness on the earth will last only a short while. Evil can never prevail over good. When it looks like the Satan is winning, always remember it is because God is about to take you to the next level of glory. When a saint is rising in glory, Satan will always try to destroy their story. The Devil may knock you down at times, but as a true believer he cannot keep you down! **Greater is He that is in me; than He that is in the world!** Satan's worst can never be greater than God's best!

"But after three and a half days, God will breathe life into them, and they stood up! Terror struck all who were starring at them. Then a loud voice from heaven called to the two prophets, "Come up here!" And they rose to heaven in a cloud as their enemies watched" (Revelation 11-13 NLT). What a scene to behold! Even as Jesus was in the grave for three days and then rose again, these two amazing witnesses will lie in the streets of Jerusalem for three and a half days. People from all over the world will stare at their dead bodies. After three and a half days, God will breathe life into them. When the enemy thought he had won, God will step in and breathe life into the two amazing witnesses. The Bible said their enemies will be terror stricken as they hear the voice of God and watch as they ascend to heaven. What glory!

"At the same time there was a terrible earthquake that destroyed a tenth of the city. Seven thousand people died in that earthquake, and everyone else was terrified and gave glory to the God of heaven" (Revelation 11:13 NLT). God will move among the people and a tenth of the city will be destroyed. Great terror will be upon the earth as God's righteousness prevails and evil is dethroned. The remnant that remains after the earthquake will give glory to the God of heaven. They will recognize the power and glory of God and repentance will take place. But after a while, they will turn against the glorious God and render their wills to Satan.

The Seventh Trumpet

"Then the seventh angel blew his trumpet, and there were loud voices shouting in heaven. 'The whole world has now become the kingdom of our Lord and of His Christ, and He will reign forever and ever'" (Revelation 11:15 NLT). What joy in heaven as the seventh trumpet is blown. Heaven begins to rejoice in the victory of the King. This was the moment all of heaven had waited to behold, the kingdoms of this world being taken out of the hand of the wicked one and restored to the King of Glory who will reign forever and ever!

The seventh trumpet will usher in the vial judgments. God is about to reign on the earth as King of Kings and Lord of Lords. No longer will there be partial judgments, but they will be complete in their destruction of all wickedness. The full measure of God's wrath will be unleashed on evil and those who refuse to accept God's plan of salvation. No one will be able to escape His judgment. **"The Lord is King forever! Let those who worship other gods be swept from the land"** (Psalm 10:16 NLT). Daniel also prophesied about this time of glory. **"As my vision continued that night, I saw someone who looked like a man coming with the clouds of heaven. He approached the Ancient One and was led into His presence. He was given authority, honor, and royal power over all the nations of the world, so that people of every race and nation and language would obey Him. His rule is eternal—it will never end. His kingdom will never be destroyed"** (Daniel 7:13-14 NLT).

"And the twenty-four elders sitting on the thrones before God fell on their faces and worshipped Him. And they said, 'We give thanks to you, Lord God Almighty, the One who is and always was, for now you have assumed your great power and have begun to reign. The nations were angry with you, but now the time of your wrath has come. It is time to judge the dead and reward your servants. You will reward your prophets and your holy people, all who fear your name, from the least to the greatest. And you will destroy all who have caused destruction on the earth'" (Revelation 11:16-18 NLT). The twenty-four elders fell on their faces in worship. They announced the coming of Christ and God having once again absolute control over His creation. He will assume His great power and begin His reign on the earth. The time has come to judge all mankind and to reward His faithful servants. The destruction of those who rebel against God's authority was certain.

The Woman and the Dragon

"Then I witnessed in heaven an event of great significance. I saw a woman clothed with the sun, with the moon beneath her feet, and a crown of twelve stars on her head" (Revelation 12:1 NLT). John saw the source of all evil. He witnessed the conflict between God and Satan. "Suddenly, I witnessed in heaven another significant event. I saw a large red dragon with seven heads and ten horns, with seven crowns on his heads. His tail dragged down one-third of the stars, which he threw to earth" (Revelation 12:3, 4a NLT). John sees Satan in all his wickedness. Can you imagine seeing Satan in all his wickedness? Satan the dragon is portrayed as a massive creature. His tail dragged one-third of the stars down to earth. Hebrew tradition tells us that these stars represent the fallen angels, those who fell with Satan and later became his demons. "His power reached to the heavens where it attacked the heavenly armies, throwing some of the heavenly beings and stars to the ground and trampling them" (Daniel 8:10 NLT).

"He stood before the woman as she was about to give birth to her child, ready to devour the baby as soon as it was born" (Revelation 12:4b NLT). John witnesses the intense struggle between righteousness and evil. It is always Satan's plan to try to thwart the plans of Jesus. He tries to frustrate you the believer so that the plans of Jesus will be aborted in your life. He is never after you but after the word of God in you, the plan of God for your life. "For I now the plans I have for you," says the Lord. "They are plans for good and not for disaster, to give you a future and a hope" (Jeremiah 29:11 NLT). Satan is a great abortionist but no match for the awesome power and glory of God. Jesus defeated Satan at every level so that the redeemed children of God may experience total freedom in life. We never have to succumb to the Devil, but we can always overcome him.

"She gave birth to a boy who was to rule all nations with an iron rod. And the child was snatched away from the dragon and was caught up to God and His throne. And the woman fled into the wilderness, where God had prepared a place to give her care for 1,260 days"

(Revelation 12:5-6 NLT). At times, like Job we may experience physical attacks from the enemy, but God will always protect His righteous seed. He will never allow Satan to destroy His church. **"For I, Myself, will be a wall of fire around Jerusalem, says the Lord. And I will be the glory inside the city!"** (Zechariah 2:5 NLT).

"Then there was war in heaven. Michael and his angels fought against the dragon and his angels. And the dragon lost the battle, and he and his angels, were forced out of heaven. This great dragon—the ancient serpent called the devil, or Satan, the one deceiving the whole world—was thrown down to the earth with all his angels" (Revelation 12:7-9 NLT). Can you imagine a war in heaven? The battle between good and evil began in heaven with Satan and a third of the angels making a futile attempt to overthrow God. It did not begin with Adam and Eve in the garden. The accuser of the brethren, that great deceiver, was forced out of heaven. His reign in the first heaven—the atmosphere above earth—had come to an end. All of the heavens along with the earth will be freed from the powers of the ancient serpent, the Devil.

"Then I heard a loud voice shouting across the heavens, 'It has come at last—salvation and power and the kingdom of our God and the authority of His Christ. For the accuser of our brothers and sisters has been thrown down to earth—the one who accuses them before our God day and night. And they have defeated him by the blood of the Lamb and by their testimony. And they did not love their lives so much that they were afraid to die. Therefore, rejoice, O heavens! And you, who live in the heavens, rejoice! But terror will come on the earth and the sea, for the devil has come down to you in great anger, knowing that he has little time'" (Revelation 12:10-12 NLT). Satan's evil hold over this earth was broken forever! He was stripped of his title as the accuser of the people of God. No longer did he have the power to dwell in the heavens. He realized that his time was short. No longer will he be the god of this world. **"Satan, who is the god of this world, has blinded the minds of those who don't believe. They are unable to see the glorious light of the Good News. They don't understand this**

message about the glory of Christ, who is the exact likeness of God" (2 Corinthians 4:4 NLT).

All of Satan's angels will be thrown down from their manning post above the earth. Every principality, powers, rulers of the darkness of this world, and spiritual wickedness in high places will be defeated. There will be no more wrestling with the forces of darkness. Satan will not be victorious on the earth. The saints of God will defeat his every attack. They will overcome him by the blood of the Lamb and their testimony. The heavens will rejoice over the downfall of Satan. Although Satan has been thrown down from the heavens, he has not been destroyed. He seeks to wreak havoc upon the earth and the sea. **"And the dragon was angry at the woman and declared war against the rest of her children—all who keep God's commandments and maintain their testimony for Jesus"** (Revelation 12:17 NLT). This will be his last futile attempt against the church of God. The church will rise up in great power against his every attack. They are glorious in their stand for Christ and will speak out boldly against the enemy, knowing that they have overcoming power through Christ's blood.

QUESTIONS FOR REVIEW

1. What happened when the seventh seal was broken?

2. How did God respond to the prayers of the saints?

3. What were the effects of the first and second trumpet judgments?

4. Describe the effects of the fourth and fifth trumpet judgments.

5. What command was given when the sixth angel blew his trumpet?

6. What were the visions given during the interlude between the sixth trumpet and the seventh trumpet?

7. In a paragraph or two, describe the two amazing witnesses and who they were believed to be.

8. How will the people of this world celebrate the death of these two witnesses?

9. What happened when the seventh trumpet was blown?

10. In chapter 12, how did the woman escape the fiery darts of the dragon?

CHAPTER TEN

The Antichrist

Revelation 13

"Then I saw a beast rising up out of the sea. It had seven heads and ten horns, with ten crowns on its horns. And written on each head were names that blasphemed God. This beast looked like a leopard, but it had the feet of a bear and the mouth of a lion! And the dragon gave the beat his own power and throne and great authority" (Revelation 13:1-2 NLT). This beast rising up out of the sea symbolizes the antichrist—the promised seed of the serpent. His nationality is known only to God. Satan gives the beast his power to reign on the earth. His purpose is not to imitate Christ but to conquer and replace Him as King of Kings and Lord of Lords. He will want to be worshiped and adored on the earth. He wants to reign from sea to sea. His purpose is to strip the earth of the glory of God for all times. He spoke blasphemies against God and waged war against the people who belonged to God.

Even now the earth is preparing for the reign of the antichrist. But Satan cannot impart his power to him until heaven says it's time. He will operate on heaven's timetable and not his own. His reign will be subject to the power of God. In Paul's letter to the churches in Thessalonica, he wrote, "For this lawlessness is already at work secretly, and it will remain secret until the one who is holding it back steps out of the way. Then the man of lawlessness will be revealed, whom the Lord Jesus will consume with the breath of His mouth and destroy by the splendor (glory) of His coming" (2 Thessalonians 2:7-8 NLT). Here Paul is talking about the spirit of the antichrist. Lawlessness is the energy behind every form of sin. And the spirit of lawlessness is subtly working in the lives of men.

Many titles are given to the antichrist. In 2 Thessalonians, Paul refers to him as the man of lawlessness, son of perdition (eternal damnation), the wicked one. "For that day will not come until there is a great rebellion against God and the man of lawlessness is revealed—the one who brings destruction. He will exalt himself and defy everything that people call god and every object of worship. He will even sit in the temple of God, claiming that he himself is God" (2 Thessalonians 2:3-4 NLT). In Daniel 7:8, he is described as the little horn. "As I was looking at the horns, suddenly another small horn appeared among them. Three of the first horns were wrenched out, roots and all, to make room for it. This little horn had eyes like human eyes and a mouth that was boasting arrogantly."

"I saw that one of the heads of the beast seemed wounded beyond recovery, but the fatal wound was healed! The entire world marveled at this miracle and followed the beast in awe. They worshipped the dragon for giving the beast such power, and they worshipped the beast. 'Is there anyone as great as the beast?' They exclaimed. 'Who is able to fight against him?' (Revelation 13:3-4 NLT). All the people of earth, whose names are not written in the Lamb's Book of Life, will worship him. He will stage a false resurrection. He will want people to see him as the Christ. The people of earth will be attracted to him because of his resemblance to the true and ever-living Christ. He will manipulate those who love evil and will eventually destroy them.

As believers, we need not despair as to his identity or even what his mark is going to be, but our concern should be the souls of men and laboring to keep hell empty of human souls. We do know from Scripture that he will be a very powerful and influential leader who will portray himself as the champion of peace. Many will be deceive by this false spirit of peace. He will appear to be able to accomplish what no other world leader is capable of doing: bringing peace to the Middle East. Daniel describes him as a warrior. "**He will become very strong, but not by his own power. He will cause a shocking amount of destruction and succeed in everything he does. He will destroy powerful leaders and devastate the holy people**" (Daniel 8:24 NLT).

During the tribulation period, his true identity will be revealed as he breaks his treaty with Israel. The antichrist will greatly influence world leaders, and will set himself up in God's temple as God. "**This evil man will come to do the work of Satan with counterfeit power and signs and miracles. He will use every kind of wicked deception to fool those who are on their way to destruction because they refuse to believe the truth that would save them**" (2 Thessalonians 2:9-10 NLT).

He will forbid the worship of God. "**For that day will not come until there is a great rebellion against God and the man of lawlessness is revealed—the one who brings destruction. He will exalt himself and defy every god there is and tear down every object of adoration and worship. He will position himself in the temple of God, claiming that he himself is God**" (2 Thessalonians 2:3b-4 NLT). But his power is limited by God. "**And he was given authority to do what he wanted for forty-two months**" (Revelation 13:15 NLT). His reign is not eternal, nor will it be greater than God's. During his reign, God will still be in absolute control of His creation. Only those who have given themselves over to evil will worship and obey the beast. "**And all the people who belonged to this world, worshipped the beast. They are the ones whose names were not written in the Book of Life, which belongs to the Lamb who was killed before the world was made**" (Revelation 13:8 NLT).

"**Then I saw another beast come up out of the earth. He had two horns like those of a lamb, and he spoke with the voice of a dragon. He exercised all the authority of the first beast. And he required all the earth and those who belonged to this world to worship the** first beast, whose death wound had been healed. He did astounding miracles, such as making fire flash down to earth from heaven while everyone was watching. And with all the miracles he was allowed to perform on behalf of the beast, he deceived all the people who belong to this world" (Revelation 13:11-14a NLT). The dragon Satan will have two accomplices: the beast of the earth and the beast of the sea. The beast of the sea is the antichrist and the beast of the earth is the false prophet. Satan will form an unholy trinity as he tries to imitate the Blessed Trinity. The antichrist, the beast of the sea, will have political power, while the false prophet, the beast of the earth, will have miraculous power. They will try in a futile attempt to overthrow God, but they themselves will be destroyed.

"He required everyone—great and small, rich and poor, slave and free—to be given a mark on the right hand or on the forehead. And no one could buy or sell anything without that mark, which was either the name of the beast or the number representing his name" (Revelation 13:16-17 NLT). The beast will seek to put to death all those who refuse to worship him and do not have his mark. The mark of the beast is 666. It is mentioned eight times in the book of Revelation. The mark will be symbolic of the beast, and his name and is associated to the number 666. Satan always tries to duplicate the acts of God. Even as God will seal His people to preserve them from this time of tribulation, Satan is requiring his people to be sealed to void his persecution upon God's people. Only those who accept the mark of the beast will be able to buy or sell. The people who accept the mark of the beast will show their loyalty to Satan and their disloyalty to God. At the appointed time, the identification of the number will be revealed.

TITLES GIVEN TO THE ANTICHRIST

There are many titles given to the antichrist in Scriptures. The names that are chosen are the ones that strongly suggest the Devilish character of this man.

Man of Sin, Son of Perdition (2 Thessalonians 2:3)—This is the most significant and revealing title of the antichrist.

King of Babylon (Isaiah 14:4)—He will oppose the principle of God's kingdom in a defiant manner.

Son of the Morning (Isaiah 14:12-15)—He will oppose God and all the seal believers on the earth.

The Man of Lawlessness (2 Thessalonians 2:8)—He represents the direct opposition of all that is righteous. Because of his lawless nature, he can be referred to as "the man of rebellion."

Lucifer (Isaiah 14:12)—Principal spirit of evil and opponent of God.

The Great Tyrannical Ruler (2 Thessalonians 2:4)—He will proclaim himself to be God.

The Little Horn (Daniel 7:8; 8:9)—The name refers to the modest (humble) political origin of the antichrist.

The Beast (Revelation 13:1)—The name depicts his horrendous persecution and slaying of the tribulation saints.

QUESTIONS FOR REVIEW

1. Who will be Satan's accomplices in his last futile attempt to overthrow God?

2. What is another name for the beast of the sea?

3. Describe the beast of the sea.

4. How did the people of this world respond to the beast?

5. What is the role of the false prophet?

6. What is the purpose of the mark of the beast?

7. List some of the names given to the antichrist.

8. How long will his power last?

CHAPTER ELEVEN

A Further Glimpse into Eternity

Revelation 14

Chapter 14 of Revelation opens with the brightness of God's glory being revealed. After such intense revelation of the overwhelming assault of evil by Satan and his helpers as they govern the earth, this glimpse into eternity is refreshing and uplifting. It reminds the believers of the reward for those who remain faithful in Christ and encourages them to press on. During the tribulation period, the antichrist will try every form of trickery and deceit to defeat the believers and get them to fall prey to his reign. But there will be those believers who will remain faithful and overcome him at every level. Some will be killed by him for not receiving his mark, but the faithful, enduring believers are seen here enjoying the benefits of heaven.

"Then I saw the Lamb standing on Mount Zion and with him were 144,000 who had His name and His Father's name written on their foreheads. And I heard the sound from heaven like the roaring of a great waterfall or the rolling of mighty thunder. It was like the sound of many harpists playing together" (Revelation 14:1-2 NLT). John's vision changes from the horrific scenes of earth to the glorious scene of heaven. Even as he saw the Lamb standing with the believers who had endured the persecution of earth, he heard the sound of glory round about them and round about the throne of God. "This choir sang a wonderful song in front of the throne of God and before the four living beings and the twenty-four elders. And no one could learn this song except those 144,000 who had been redeemed from the earth" (Revelation 14:3 NLT).

These 144,000 represent the entrenched followers of the Lamb of glory. They willingly followed the Lamb wherever He went. "For they are spiritually undefiled, pure as virgins, following the Lamb wherever He goes. They have been purchased from among the people on the earth as a special offering to God and to the Lamb" (Revelation 14:4 NLT). They represent the believers who endured the persecution and hardship of earth and refused to give up on their faith. They are seen here reaping the glorious recompense and blessings of heaven. These believers kept their righteous robes on in the face of adversity. They did not love their own lives more than their faith and life in Christ. They were spiritually pure and deserving of the pleasures of heaven.

As a believer, you may have to suffer unjustly at times, but never allow it to soil your righteous garment. All unjust suffering is always a righteous suffering and your day of recompense will come. "Dear friends, don't be surprised at the fiery trials you are going through, as if something strange were happening to you. Instead, be very glad—because these trails will make you partners with Christ in His suffering, and afterward you will have the wonderful joy of sharing His glory when it is displayed to the world" (1 Peter 4:12-13 NLT). "But it is no shame to suffer for being a Christian. Praise God for the privilege of being called by His wonderful name!" (1 Peter 4:16 NLT). "God blesses you when you are mocked and persecuted and lied about because you are My followers. Be happy about it! Be very glad! For a great reward awaits you in heaven" (Matthew 5:11-12 NLT).

John's attention was then turned to three angels that were flying through the heavens. Each of them had an announcement of great importance for the inhabitants of earth. The first carried the message of the everlasting gospel. The second announcement was that of the fall of Babylon, that evil and immoral empire, and the third was a proclamation of destruction for those who worship the beast and receive his mark.

"And I saw another angel flying through the heavens, carrying the everlasting Good News to preach to the people who belong to this world—to every nation, tribe, language, and people. 'Fear God,' he shouted. 'Give glory to Him. For the time has come when He will sit as Judge. Worship Him who made heaven and earth, the sea, and all the springs of water' (Revelation 14:6-7 NLT). This is an announcement of God's great judgment that is about to begin.

It can also be considered as a final appeal to all mankind—every tribe, nation, language, and people—to repent, to turn to God. God created man to give him glory and those who refuse to fear and worship Him will be judged by Him on that great day. **"The Lord Almighty says, 'The day of judgment is coming, burning like a furnace. The arrogant and the wicked will be burned up like straw on that day. They will be consumed like a tree—roots and all. But for you who fear my name, the Sun of Righteousness will rise with healing in His wings. And you will go free, leaping with joy like calves let out to pasture. On the day when I act, you will tread upon the wicked as if they were dust under your feet,' says the Lord Almighty"** (Malachi 4:1-3 NLT).

"Then another angel followed him through the skies, shouting, 'Babylon is fallen—that great city is fallen—because she seduced the nations of the world and made them drink the wine of her passionate immorality'" (Revelation 14:8 NLT). The proclamation here suggests to us that even as Babylon was known as a wicked, immoral city, all that is religiously, politically, and commercially corrupt will fall. On that great day, man's power will be no match for the power of God. It will not survive the wrath of God's anger upon the earth. **"Then a third angel followed them, shouting, 'Anyone who worships the beast and his statue or who accepts his mark on the forehead or the hand must drink the wine of God's wrath. It is poured out undiluted into God's cup of wrath'** (Revelation 14:9-10 NLT).

The wrath of God will be experienced by all the worshippers of the beast, both great and small. The wine of God's wrath will be full-strength. All the inhabitants of earth who rejected God and accepted the mark of the beast will drink full strength of the wine from God's cup of fury. Their torment will be eternal. **"And they will be tormented with fire and burning sulfur in the presence of the holy angels and the Lamb. The smoke of their torment rises forever and ever, and they will have no relief day or night, for they have worshipped the beast and his statue and have accepted the mark of his name"** (Revelation 10b-11 NLT).

"Let this encourage God's holy people to endure persecution patiently and remain firm to the end, obeying His commands and trusting in Jesus" (Revelation 14:12 NLT). God's ultimate victory serves as a means of encouragement to the tribulation saints to remain faithful. Trust God in the midst of trials and persecution. Don't give in and despair; keep your eyes on Jesus who is the Author and Finisher of your faith. **"We do this by keeping our eyes on Jesus, on whom our faith depends from start to finish. Think about all He endured when sinful people did such terrible things to Him, so that you don't become weary and give up"** (Hebrews 12:2a; 3 NLT).

"And I heard a voice from heaven saying, 'Write this down: Blessed are those who die in the Lord from now on. Yes, says the Spirit, they are blessed indeed, for they will rest from all their toils and trials; for their good deeds will follow them!'" (Revelation 14:13 NLT). Heaven announces a blessing upon the saints who will die because of their faithfulness during the time of God judgment on the earth. The tribulation saints will go through much hardship and persecution. It will not be an easy time for the faithful worshippers of God. But there will be a day of recompense.

The overcoming saints will be rewarded from all their toils and trials. The Bible says that their good deeds will follow them. Only what is done for Christ will last. Their material wealth and worldly accomplishments will be left behind, but every work for the kingdom will follow the worker in death.

"Then I saw the Son of Man sitting on a white cloud. He had a gold crown on His head and a sharp sickle in His hand. Then an angel came from the temple and called out in a loud voice to the One sitting on the cloud, 'Use the sickle, for the time has come for you to harvest; the crop is ripe on the earth.' So the One sitting on the cloud swung His sickle over the earth, and the whole earth was harvested" (Revelation 14:14-16 NLT). This is a picture of God's judgment of the earth. The martyr's cry for righteous revenge is about to take place. Christ Jesus, the King of all Kings and the Lord of all Lords, will reap the harvest. He will avenge the blood of the martyrs.

The people of earth who rejected God's plan of salvation and worshipped the beast will be gathered like clusters of grapes and then crushed into the great winepress of God's wrath. "So the angel swung his sickle on the earth and loaded the grapes into the great winepress of God's wrath" (Revelation 14:19 NLT). The prophet Isaiah wrote, "In my anger I have trampled my enemies as if they were grapes. In my fury I have trampled my foes. It is their blood that has stained my clothes" (Isaiah 62:3 NLT).

QUESTIONS FOR REVIEW

1) Who did the 144,000 on Mount Zion represent?

2) What were the announcements that were carried by the three angels?

3) Who will experience God's cup of wrath?

4) What is said about the overcoming saints?

5) What will happen to the people of earth who rejected God's plan of salvation?

6) How will the overcoming saints be rewarded?

CHAPTER TWELVE

The Seven Bowls of the Seven Plagues

Revelation 15-16

"Then I saw in heaven another significant event, and it was great and marvelous. Seven angels were holding the seven last plagues, which would bring God's wrath to completion. I saw before me what seemed to be a crystal sea mixed with fire. And on it stood all the people who had been victorious over the beast and his statue and the number representing his name. They were holding harps that God had given them" (Revelation 15:1-2 NLT). This chapter opens with John seeing another important event in heaven. He describes it as being great and marvelous, an amazing event. John saw seven angels holding the seven last plagues that will complete God's judgment of earth. The angels stood ready to pour out the seven last plagues. Nothing and no one can hold back the completion of God's wrath. They awaited the command of God in this final act of judgment on the earth.

John also saw the overcoming tribulation saints in worship. They were holding harps that were given to them by God and were singing the triumphant song of Moses and the Lamb. "**And they were singing the**

song of Moses, the servant of God, and the song of the Lamb: Great
and marvelous are your actions, Lord God Almighty. Just and true
are your ways, O King of the nations. Who will not fear, O Lord, and
glorify your name? For you alone are holy. All nations will come and
worship before you. For your righteous deeds have been revealed"
(Revelation 15:3-4 NLT). These overcoming tribulation saints were in
the glory giving God glory.

They were worshipping before the throne of God. Can you imagine
their joy and expressions of praise for triumphing over the beast? There
is always inexpressible gratitude when you have gone through much
and come out on top. You give to God continuous praise and adoration
because you realize He kept you even when Satan tried his best to
conquer and destroy you. These saints had triumphed against great odds
and overcome the terrors of the tribulation period by not worshipping
the beast. They stood strong in the faith and overcame him (Satan).
"And they have defeated him because of the blood of the Lamb and
because of their testimony" (Revelation 12:11 NLT).

"Then I looked and saw that the temple in heaven, God's Tabernacle,
was thrown wide open! The seven angels who were holding the bowl
of the seven plagues came from the temple, clothed in spotless white
linen with gold belts across their chests" (Revelation 15:5-6 NLT).
This was a direct imagery of the tabernacle that God told Moses to build
in the wilderness. We can now understand why God told Moses to make
the tabernacle and its furnishing precisely according to His plans. "I
want the people of Israel to build me a sacred residence where I can
live among them. You must make this Tabernacle and its furnishing
exactly according to the plans I will show you" (Exodus 25:8 NLT).
It was a replica of this heavenly tabernacle where the ark of the covenant
(God's divine presence among His people) resided. Now John was seeing
the actual tabernacle being opened in heaven. The seven angels that came
from the tabernacle were dressed in spotless white linen with gold belts
across their chests. Their apparel was similar to that of the High Priest
and showed their purity from sin.

"And one of the four living beings handed each of the seven angels a gold bowl filled with the terrible wrath of God, who lives forever and ever" (Revelation 15:7 NLT). One of the four living beings handed each of the angels a gold bowl that was filled with the dreadful wrath of God. The bowls of the last seven plagues were ready to be poured out on those who rejected God's Word and law. There will be no escaping God's judgment on this world. Every person who cast off God's Word and law will experience the judgment of God.

The eternal reign of God is once again established in John's revelation. "Who lives forever and ever" (Revelation 15:7 NLT). God, not Satan, has eternal power that can never be diminished. The plans of the Satan to confuse, to befuddle you is temporary. "This too shall pass." Only God and His Word are eternal. Don't become strained by Satan's plans for your life, but trust the eternal plans and the hand of God.

"The Temple was filled with smoke from God's glory and power. No one could enter the Temple until the seven angels had completed pouring out the seven plagues" (Revelation 15:8 NLT). When God gives a command, He supports it with His glory and power. Nothing is able to stand in its way. The command shall come to pass. John saw the manifested power and glory of God filling the temple. No one who has the mark of the beast or worships his statue will be able to escape the seven bowl judgments.

The First Bowl Judgment

"Then I heard a mighty voice shouting from the Temple to the seven angels, 'Now go your ways and empty out the seven bowls of God's wrath on the earth'" (Revelation 16:1 NLT). The angels were commanded to go and carry out God's final judgments on the earth. These judgments are more complete and severe than the previous ones. The unbelievers will all perish in this final judgment. "So the first angel left the Temple and poured out his bowl over the earth, and horrible, malignant sores broke out on everyone who had the mark of the

beast and who worshipped his statue" (Revelation 16:2 NLT). The first angel bowl was poured out over the earth and every worshipper of the antichrist, the worshippers of his statue, and all those with the mark of the beast were smitten with incurable sores. These sores were nasty, unbearable, and incurable. This judgment was just the first of the seven that will afflict the lives of all those who rejected Christ.

The Second Bowl Judgment

"Then the second angel poured out his bowl on the sea, and it became like the blood of a corpse. And everything in the sea died" (Revelation 16:3 NLT). Can you imagine everything in the sea dying? There will be no sea life anywhere. All sea life will be destroyed by this second bowl judgment. Every sea will be contaminated and have the appearance of blood. What an awful stench that will be coming forth from the bloody sea and the diseases that will accompany it! This second bowl judgment will cause a global upheaval. It will complete what the second trumpet judgment had started. Fishing, sea transportation, and shipping will all be affected by this judgment. The doors of earth will be coming to a close and heaven's doors will be opening on the earth. What glory!

The Third Bowl Judgment

"Then the third angel poured out his bowl on the rivers and springs, and they became blood. And I heard the angel who had authority over all water saying, 'You are just in sending this judgment, O holy One who is and who always was. For your holy people and your prophets have been killed, and their blood was poured out on the earth. So you have given their murderers blood to drink. It is their just reward.' And I heard a voice from the altar saying; 'Yes Lord God Almighty, your punishments are true and just' (Revelation 16:4-7 NLT). The inhabitants of earth will be forced to drink bloody water. There will be no pure drinking water on the earth. The wealthiest man on the earth will not be able to buy pure water to survive this judgment.

Money will not help secure drinking or bathing water. The thought of being thirsty and not being able to obtain drinking water is nerve racking. Through this judgment, the vengeance of the martyred saints was taking place on the earth. The martyred saints behind the altar were waiting for this day. They joined the angel who had authority over the waters in worship of God. God is the Great Avenger of the faith. At times it may seem as though He is letting your enemies get away, but He has a day of recompense for the righteous, a day when you will be rewarded and your enemies will pay for their deeds. "**For we know the One who said, 'I will take vengeance. I will repay those who deserve it'**" (Hebrews 10:30a NLT).

The Fourth Bowl Judgment

Then the fourth angel poured out his bowl on the sun, causing it to scorch everyone with its fire. Everyone was burned by this blast of heat, and they cursed the name of God, who sent all these plagues. They did not repent and give Him glory" (Revelation 16:8-9 NLT). This plague will intensify the heat of the sun to a degree where it will sear and burn the skin of mankind everywhere. Even the north and south poles will be places of intense heat. Those of us who live in the region of the equator know what it is like to experience the heat of the noonday sun at summertime. But this plague is indescribably worse. No one will be able to escape its rays and no cooling system will be able to lend support. There will be no hiding place from the blast of this heat. But just like the Pharaoh of Moses' time, the worshippers of the beast will refuse to repent; rather they will curse the name of God.

The Fifth Bowl Judgment

"**Then the fifth angel poured out his bowl on the throne of the beast, and his kingdom was plunged into darkness. And his subjects ground their teeth in anguish, and they cursed the God of heaven for their pains and sores. But they refuse to repent of all their evil deeds**"

(Revelation 16:10-11 NLT). The kingdom of the beast will be thrown into confusion by this judgment. His worshippers will be overcome with torture and pain, but they will refuse to repent. They will curse God for their discomfort and misery but will not give up their evil deeds. Their hearts will be hardened against the tender mercies of God.

In John's revelation, the earth was in its final stages of delivery. The cosmic war was now at a glory peak. This earth's purging was near completion. Evil was being wiped out for all times. The worshippers of the beast were covered in incurable, painful sores. There was no drinking water to be found. All the waters were turned to blood. All sea life had been destroyed and the sun was pouring down searing heat upon the men and women who were already suffering from the malignant sores. The beast had been dethroned and his kingdom covered in darkness. No man (no matter how powerful) will be able to help the next. This will be the judgment where the hard, stubborn roots of sin will be pulled up out of the earth, never to be replanted. This is the final judgment of God upon all those who worship the beast. Where will you be when this horrendous judgment is taking place?

The Sixth Bowl Judgment

"Then the sixth angel poured out his bowl on the great Euphrates River, and it dried up so that the kings from the east could march their armies westward without hindrance. And I saw three evil spirits that look like frogs leap from the mouth of the dragon, the beast, and the false prophet. These miracle working-demons caused all the rulers of the world to gather for battle against the Lord on that great judgment day of God Almighty" (Revelation 16:12-14 NLT). The sixth bowl judgment made the way ready for the final war of the age by drying up the great Euphrates River. The armies of the world will march unhindered to accompany the antichrist to battle against God. The nations will be deceived; they will be demonized by the miracle-working demons that will come out of the mouth of the dragon—Satan (the beast), the antichrist, and the false prophet. These evil spirits will entice the nations to join forces with Satan, the antichrist and the false prophet, in supporting evil and a last futile attempt against the sovereign God and His kingdom. The entire world will be plunge into mass destruction by these evil spirits.

"Take note: I will come as unexpectedly as a thief! Blessed are all who are watching for me, who keep their robes ready so they will not need to walk naked and ashamed" (Revelation 16:15 NLT). We the readers are warned once again by Christ to be ready for His imminent return. Even as John was witnessing the happenings of the sixth bowl judgment, there came a warning to the church community to keep our robes ready (righteous deeds) so that we will not be found naked and ashamed upon His return. **"Blessed are all who are watching for me, who keep their robes ready so they will not need to walk naked and ashamed"** (Revelation 16:15b NLT).

"And they gathered all the rulers and their armies to a place called Armageddon in Hebrew" (Revelation 16:16 NLT). The wicked nations of this world will unite with Satan, the antichrist, and the false prophet to war against God and His people at a place call Armageddon.

The Seventh Bowl Judgment

"Then the seventh angel poured out his bowl into the air. And a mighty shout came from the throne of the Temple in heaven, saying, 'It is finished!' Then the thunder crashed and rolled, and lightning flashed. And there was an earthquake greater than ever before in human history. The great city of Babylon split into three pieces, and cities around the world fell into heaps of rubble" (Revelation 16:17-19 NLT). With the pouring out of the seventh bowl, there will be a mighty shout from heaven's throne saying, "It is finished!" This judgment will bring conclusion to the period known as the great tribulation. Earth was about to experience massive destruction greater than any other from the beginning of time. Human history (as we know it) was about to come to an end. The eternal glory reign was about to begin on the earth.

Babylon and all the cities around the world will fall into heaps of rubble; the islands will disappear and every mountain will be leveled. But the people of earth will still continue to curse God and turn to Him. "And so God remembered all of Babylon's sins, and he made her drink the cup that was filled with the wine of His fierce wrath. And every island disappeared, and all the mountains were leveled. There was a terrible hailstorm, and hailstones weighing seventy-five pounds fell from the sky on the people below. They cursed God because of the hailstorm, which was a very terrible plague" (Revelation 16:16-21 NLT).

QUESTIONS FOR REVIEW

1. According to verses 1-2, what was the event John saw in heaven?

2. What was the song that was being sung by the overcoming tribulation saints?

3. Describe the first bowl judgment?

4. How did the second bowl judgment affect the sea?

5. What happened when the third bowl judgment was poured out?

6. How will the fourth bowl judgment affect the heat of the sun?

7. What happened to the throne of the beast when the fifth bowl judgment is poured out?

8. Describe the effects of the seventh bowl judgment?

CHAPTER THIRTEEN

The Great Prostitute

Revelation 17-18

"One of the seven angels who had poured out the seven bowls came over and spoke to me. 'Come with me,' he said, 'And I will show you the judgment that is going to come on the great prostitute, who sits on many waters. The rulers of the world have had immoral relations with her, and the people who belong to this world have been made drunk by the wine of her immorality'" (Revelation 17:1-2 NLT). The great prostitute represents "The Place Where Satan Lives," which is known as religious Babylon. It is a place of great spiritual wickedness. It also represents every religion, person, government, and manner of false religion and apostate Christianity.

Note the sharp dissimilarities between the great prostitute and the bride of Christ.

The Great Prostitute	The Bride of Christ
1. Ruled by Satan	Ruled by Christ
2. Clothed in evil	Clothed in glory
3. A carrier of Satan's power	A carrier of God's power

4. Leads people into evil   Leads people into righteousness

5. A lover of Satan   A lover of God

6. Advancing the kingdom of Satan Advancing the kingdom of God

7. Eternal destination is hell Eternal destination is heaven

The great prostitute will sway many religions and nations into wickedness. The name Babylon comes from the word *Babel*—a scene or place of noisy confusion. It represents false religion, witchcraft, sorcery, astrology, and every other devilish rebellion against God.

The great prostitute along with the nations will give their power and authority to the beast that was alive who will come up out of the bottomless pit. All the people of this world whose names are not written in the Lamb's Book of Life will be in awe at his reappearance. They will give their power and authority to him and together they will war against the Lamb, but they will be defeated by Him who is the Lord of Lords and the King of Kings. **"Together they will wage war against the Lamb, but the Lamb will defeat them because He is Lord over all lords and King over all kings, and His people are the called and chosen and faithful ones"** (Revelation 17:14 NLT).

"And the angel said to me, 'The waters where the prostitute is sitting represent masses of people of every nation and language. The scarlet beast and his ten horns (which represent the ten kings who will reign with him) all hate the prostitute. They will strip her naked, eat her flesh, and burn her remains with fire. For God has put a plan into their minds, a plan that will carry out his purposes" (Revelation 17:15-17a NLT). God will use people who are against Him to carry out His plans on the earth. The very people who worked with the great prostitute turned on her and destroyed her. God placed a plan into the people's mind. Once God has placed a plan in motion, nothing is able to stop or destroy it. God's plan will come to fruition. In our lives, we must always trust the plans that God has concerning us. His plans are more powerful than any plans of Satan. **"For I know the plans I have**

for you," says the Lord. "They are plans for good and not disaster, to give you a future and a hope" (Jeremiah 29:11 NLT).

"After all this I saw another angel come down from heaven with great authority, and the earth grew bright with his splendor. He gave a mighty shout, 'Babylon is fallen—that great city is fallen!'" (Revelation 18:1-2a NLT). This world system (as we know it) will fall. Everything around us that is controlled by evil and bears the label of the Devil will be destroyed. Everything that opposes God's purposes will come to an aggressive end. There will be massive destruction with the falling of Babylon. The people of earth will lose everything that they have worked a lifetime to secure. It will be taken away in a single hour. The Babylons of our life will fall, and what a fall that will be! Let us not live and labor feverishly for material gain; it will profit us nothing in eternity. But let us labor for the kingdom of God that will provide a place of rest in eternity. "Let heaven fill your thoughts. Do not think only about things down here on earth" (Colossians 3:2 NLT).

QUESTIONS FOR REVIEW

1. What does the great prostitute represent?

2. List the sharp similarities of the great prostitute and the bride of Christ?

3. Where does the name Babylon come from?

4. Who will the great prostitute and the nations worship?

5. Who will destroy the great prostitute and how?

6. What will happen when Babylon falls?

CHAPTER FOURTEEN

Rapid Glory!

Revelation 19

Heaven's Hallelujah Chorus

"After this, I heard the sound of a vast crowd in heaven shouting, 'Hallelujah! Salvation is from our God. Glory and power belong to Him alone. His judgments are just and true. He has punished the great prostitute who corrupted the earth with her immorality, and He has avenged the murder of His servants.' Again and again their voices rang, "Hallelujah! The smoke from that city ascends forever and ever!"" (Revelation 19:1-3 NLT). There was a great celebration in heaven. The vast crowd in heaven rejoices, shouting praises of hallelujah. This was the time that all of creation waited for—the final victory over evil. The cosmic war against good and evil was quickly coming to a victorious end. Good had prevailed over evil. This earth was once again being clothed in the splendor of God's glory. The reign of Jesus Christ, the paschal Lamb as the King of Kings and Lord of Lords over all the kingdoms of this world, was about to begin. God's divine rule was being established forever and ever.

"Then the twenty-four elders and four living beings fell down and worshipped God, who was sitting on the throne. They cried out,

'Amen! Hallelujah!' (Revelation 19:4 NLT). The heavenly hosts join in the hallelujah chorus. The word *hallelujah* is mentioned four times in this passage. It originates from two Hebrew words: *halal*, meaning "praise" and *Jah* meaning "Yahweh" or "Lord." The hosts of heaven were in high praise for the splendor of God's glory had risen and He was about to cover the earth as the water covers the sea. They cried, "So be it! Praise the Lord!"

Every time the church says, "Hallelujah," we are giving God the highest praise. It sums up everything about praise. "Praise the Lord!" When it seems like you cannot get a breakthrough, open your mouth and begin to bless the Lord with the hallelujah chorus. "Hallelujah! Praise the Lord, Hallelujah! Praise the Lord, Hallelujah! Praise the Lord. (Are you getting it?) The Devil hates a hallelujah believer. Every hallelujah that makes its way into the heavens frustrates the plans of the enemy.

The Devil needs to hear a clear sound coming from the church of God. "Hallelujah!" If hallelujah is great praise for heaven, imagine what it will accomplish on the earth. When you are in pain, *Hallelujah!* When you are becoming distress, *Hallelujah!* When you don't know what to do and it seems like your faith is failing you, *Hallelujah* your way through! Hallelujah is one of your greatest innate weapons against the Devil. It is one of the best kept secrets to overcoming the wicked schemes of the Devil. *Hallelujah* him out of your way!

"And from the throne came a voice that said, 'Praise our God, all His servants, from the least to the greatest, all who fear Him'" (Revelation 19:5 NLT). The voice summons all of God's servants to join the heavenly host in the hallelujah chorus. The praise of God echoed throughout the heavens and earth. What a glorious celebration! There was rejoicing, adoration, thanksgiving, praise, and worship. It was all glory and more glory. Can you imagine what a sound that will be when all of the heavenly hosts, saints of the ages, and the redeemed church get together in celebration of the dethroning of Satan and his powers and the reign of glory on the earth? There will be no end to this glorious worship.

Nothing will be able to compare to the sound of glory that will come from the creatures for the Creator!

The power and glory of God was now reigning throughout creation. The saints in heaven and earth were rejoicing. It was truly a hallelujah time! We can't ignore the "Hallelujah Chorus" that was written by George Frederic Handel in 1741; he did a great job. It was a work of art. But the hallelujah chorus in heaven was like the sound of many waters. John could not accurately describe this sound. He used symbols that we the readers could understand. **"Then I heard again what sounded like a shout of a huge crowd, or the roar of mighty ocean waves, or the crash of loud thunder: Hallelujah! For the Lord our God, the Almighty reigns"** (Revelation 19:6 NLT).

The Marriage Supper of the Lamb

"Let us be glad and rejoice, and let us give honor to Him. For the time has come for the wedding feast of the Lamb, and His bride has prepared herself. She has been given the finest of pure white linen to wear. For the fine linen represents the good deeds (righteousness) of God's holy people" (Revelation 19:7, 8 NLT). The Bible tells us about a marriage supper of the Lamb. It tells us about the marriage of the Lamb and then the supper. When this event was shown to John, he had to use symbols that we the readers could understand. Jesus talked about being ready for the Bridegroom's return. In Matthew 25 when talking about the coming kingdom of God, He gives us the parable of the "Ten Bridesmaids." He pointed out the folly of the five foolish virgins who were not ready for the marriage feast.

In Revelation 9:10-13, we are reminded that only those who have prepared themselves will be partakers of the wedding feast of the Lamb. **"Then those who were ready went in with Him to the marriage feast, and the door was locked. Later, when the other five bridesmaids returned, they stood outside, calling, 'Lord! Lord! Open the door for us!' But He called back, *'Believe me, I don't know you!'* So you,**

too, must keep watch! For you do not know the day or hour of My return."

The marriage of the Lamb will take place in heaven at the end of the tribulation and just before the reign of Christ upon the earth. What a glorious time it will be! The bride and the guests of Christ are all those who stood the test and went from faith to faith during their glory journey on the earth. All the saints of the ages will make up His bride. It will be a gathering of the saints, that glorious church without spot or wrinkle, who have made themselves ready. John does not describe the marriage; he only announces it. Nowhere in Scriptures is there a description of the marriage of the Lamb. But we do have a description of the bride.

I) **"She has been given the finest of pure white linen to wear"** (Revelation 19:8a NLT). The appearance of the bride will be glorious, beyond words. The pure white linen is symbolic of the purity of God, our righteous living on the earth. We are to live upright before God on the earth. The *Life Application Study Bible Commentary* states, "The bride's clothing represents the good deeds of the believers. These good deeds are not done by believers to their merit, but they reflect the work of Christ to save us."

II) **"She will be holy and without fault"** (Ephesians 5:27b NLT). A life that is free from the love of sin. God has made provision through Jesus for His bride to be holy and without fault. Through His blood, we have been cleansed from sin and set apart for His glory. **"So also Jesus suffered and died outside the city gates to make His people holy by means of His own blood"** (Hebrews 13:12 NLT).

III) The bride will be glorious, clothed in the righteousness of God. **"A glorious Church without spot or wrinkle or any other blemish"** (Ephesians 5:27a NLT).

The marriage takes place in heaven. The bride will be dressed in the righteous robe of God. She will be gloriously attired. Isaiah wrote, **"I am overwhelmed with joy in the Lord my God! For He has dressed me with the clothing of salvation and draped me in a robe of righteousness"** (Isaiah 61:10a NLT). The Bible says that God has imputed His righteousness to His bride through Jesus Christ. **"God made Him who had no sin to be sin for us, so that in Him we might become the righteousness of God"** (2 Corinthians 5:21 NIV). The good deeds (righteous acts, motives) of the bride will serve as the bridal garment. As believers, we are to prepare ourselves for the marriage of the Lamb by being clothed in the righteousness of God in all seasons of our lives. We are to live the life that God has chosen for us and not the life that we have chosen for ourselves. **"The steps of a good (righteous) man are ordered by the Lord: and He delighteth in his ways"** (Psalm 37:23 KJV).

"And the angel said, 'Write this: Blessed are those who are invited to the wedding feast of the Lamb.' And he added, 'These are true words that come from God' (Revelation 19:9 NLT). The church along with Old Testament and New Testament saints has been invited by Christ to the marriage feast of the Lamb. We are the invited guests and the bride of Christ. We are among the blessed ones to whom the invitation has been extended. We accept the invitation by being obedient to His righteous standard of life.

When we gave our life to Christ, a contract was signed. We became engaged to Him. We made the commitment to live for Him. We promised to serve Him in true obedience. Our love, obedience, and service to Him will dress us for the marriage supper when the great consummation will take place. He will come to take His ready bride away to His place of abode. After the marriage celebration, there will be a honeymoon. We will return to earth to reign with Him for a thousand years. What a honeymoon!

The entire community of believers, all the saints of the ages, is invited to the wedding feast of the Lamb. The Old Testament and the New

Testament saints will be there. The tribulation saints will be there. All those who remain faithful will be in attendance. The entire major and minor prophets—Abraham, Isaac, Jacob, Moses, and David (just to name a few)—will be there. We will all be married to Christ for all eternity. As His bride, we are called upon to dress ourselves in fine linen (the righteousness of God). Every saint of the ages who has prepared himself or herself in fine linen will become the bride of Christ. We will be the wife who has made herself ready. "When He shall come with trumpet sound, O may I then in Him be found. Dressed in His righteousness alone; Faultless to stand before the throne" (Edward Mote, "On Christ the Solid Rock I Stand," 1834).

Heaven's Rewards

Bible scholars have concluded that it is at this time that the believers work will be tried and rewards will be given. The time is really not important. But we do know from Scriptures that our work will be tried and we will be rewarded. There will be a believers' judgment. As believers, we can never earn these rewards, but they are given to those who remain faithful and true to the cross of Christ. The believers' judgment will be quite different from the Great White Throne judgment. As believers, we will all stand before Christ to be judged. We will be rewarded for how we have lived. **"For we must all stand before Christ to be judged. We will each receive whatever we deserve for the good or evil we have done in our bodies"** (2 Corinthians 5:10 NLT).

Our motives will be put on trial; they will go through the tester and only what was done with purity of heart will pass the test. **"But there is going to come a time of testing at the judgment day to see what kind of work each builder has done. Everyone's work will be put through the fire to see whether or not it keeps its value. If the work survives the fire, that builder will receive a reward. But if the work is burned up, the builder will suffer great loss. The builders themselves will be saved, but like someone escaping through a wall of flames"** (1 Corinthians 3:13-15 NLT). Our work will be tried and only what was done with the right motive will pass the test. It's true that only what was done for Christ will last. Our work could look really good to those around us, but will it survive the fire when it is tried? Will it keep its value?

Each person will be rewarded according to how well he has completed his God-given assignment. Your pursuit of God down here will determine your reward up there. Paul said that for those whose work is burned up, they will be saved as though fleeing through a burning fire. If your work survives the fire, you will be rewarded. Your work must be done out of a heart of love. Your love for God should always be the compelling force behind your labor in the kingdom. The work that comes forth from such a loving heart will be able to endure the tester's fire.

Heaven's rewards are not something you can earn. They are a gift of God's grace. The believers of the church age will be rewarded according to their obedience to the work of the cross of Jesus. **"If any of you wants to be my followers, you must put aside selfish ambition, shoulder your cross, and follow me. If you try to keep your life for yourself, you will lose it. But if you give up your life for me, you will find true life"** (Matthew 16:24-25 NLT). Your reward will be determined by your faithfulness to the cross of Jesus. If it was done as a follower of Christ, it will last. If it was done for selfish gain, it will be destroyed by the fire. Jessie Pounds, a hymn writer, was focused on being Jesus' disciple, His follower, when she wrote "The Way of the Cross Leads Home."

The Believers' Crowns

"Look I am coming quickly. Hold on to what you have, so that no one will take away your crown" (Revelation 3:11 NLT). The church in Philadelphia was told to hold on to its faith that its crown will not be taken away. The crowns will be given to those who faithfully endured and overcame the world, flesh, and the Devil.

There are five crowns that are available to loyal believers in Christ.

1) **The Crown of Life**—"Remain faithful even when facing death and I will give you the crown of life" (Revelation 2:10 NLT). The crown of life is the overcomer's crown. It is given to believers who triumph over the plans of the Devil. We must remain faithful and resist the Devil at every level. "**God blesses the people who patiently endure testing. Afterward they will receive the crown of life that God has promised to those who love Him**" (James 1:12 NLT). The crown of life has been promised by God to the overcoming believers. The time of hard testing will come, but press your way through; there is a reward awaiting you.

2) **The Incorruptible Crown**—"**Everyone who competes in the game goes into strict training. They do it to get a crown that will not last; but we do it to get a crown that will last forever**" (1 Corinthians 9:25 NLT). It is known as the disciplined crown, the crown of distinction. This crown will be given to all those believers who overcome the desire of the flesh and exercise self-control in this present life. All those who strive for distinction in their relationship with Christ will receive the crown of distinction known as the incorruptible crown.

3) **Crown of Righteousness**—"**I have fought a good fight, I have finished the race, and I have remained faithful. And now the prize awaits me—the crown of righteousness that the Lord, the Righteous Judge, will give me on that great day of His return. And the prize is not just for me, but for all who eagerly look forward to His glorious return**" (2 Timothy 4:7-8 NLT). The crown of righteousness will be given to all those who finish their course, their God-given assignment. The church will have to give an account of what it did with its God-given assignment. Sad to say, there will be a lot of believers whose assignments will be graded incomplete. We must strive to do what God has assigned and not what we want to do for His kingdom. The crown of righteousness will be given to those who eagerly look forward to Christ's return—the ready and

waiting bride of Christ will receive this crown. We must strive to finish the course. **"I strain to reach the end of the race and receive the prize for which God, through Christ Jesus, is calling us up to heaven"** (Philippians 3:14 NLT).

4) Crown of Rejoicing—**"For what is our hope, our joy, or the crown in which we will glory in the presence of our Lord Jesus when He comes? Is it not you? Indeed, you are our glory and joy"** (1 Thessalonians 2:19 NLT). This crown of rejoicing is the soul winner's crown. The Scriptures tell us that He who wins souls is wise (Proverbs 11:30). If we go after souls, snatching them from the very gates of hell, our reward will be the crown of rejoicing. In heaven, we will be rejoicing all the time. The souls that you witness to and will be in heaven with you, even those to whom you witness but did not repent will qualify you for this crown. Have you witnessed recently? **"Show mercy to those whose faith is wavering. Rescue others by snatching them from the flames of judgment"** (Jude 22-23a NLT).

5) Crown of Glory—**"Be shepherds of God's flock that is under your care, serving as overseers—not because you must, but because you are willing, as God wants you to be, not greedy for money, but eager to serve; not lording over those entrusted to you, but being examples to the flock. And when the Chief Shepherd appears, you will receive the crown of glory that will never fade away"** (1 Peter 5:2-4 NIV). Leaders are accountable to God for His flocks. The crown of glory will be given to spiritual leaders who prove themselves faithful in their labor and maintain God's righteous standard in their ministry. This crown will be given to those who serve with a pure heart. He will reward His leaders for the great sacrifice that has to be made by them in shepherding His flocks. Every spiritual leader should strive for the crown of glory.

There will be a coronation at the marriage supper of the Lamb. We the saints of the ages will willingly lay our crowns at Jesus' feet. We will acknowledge Him as King of Kings and Lord of Lords. We will show gratitude for all Jesus has done for us: the grace and mercy that were shown to us during our earthly pilgrimage and the blood covering that provided safety from the storms of life. Yes, we will crown Him Lord of all! We will join Edward Perronet in his rendition of "All Hail the Power of Jesus' Name!" whose lyrics include "Let angels prostrate fall; bring forth the royal diadem, and crown Him Lord of all." With joy, much joy, we will crown Him King of Kings and Lord of all!

The question for you is this: How well are you running this Christian race? Will you finish your course? Will you receive a crown? After this life with all its struggles and disappointments, will you be a part of this time of celebration in heaven, the marriage supper of the Lamb? What will happen when your work is tried? Will it survive the Tester's fire?

The Battle of Armageddon

"Then I saw heaven opened, and a white horse was standing there. Its rider was named Faithful and True, for He judges fairly and wages a righteous war. His eyes were like flames of fire, and on His head were many crowns. A name was written on Him that no one understood except Himself. He wore a robe dipped in blood, and His title was the Word of God" (Revelation 19:11-13 NLT). Once again John saw heaven opened. He was not about to enter heaven as we saw in chapter 4, but Jesus is about to return to earth not as a Lamb but as a Warrior, Conqueror, and the King of Glory. He will not return through the womb of a woman to die on a cruel cross, but He will return in all His glory to reign as King of Kings and Lord of Lords.

John describes for his readers the rider on the white horse that was about to be dispatch from heaven. He was seeing Jesus as the Great Commander, the Defender of the Faith ready for battle. It appears that John was having some difficulty describing the power and the glory in the person of Jesus that he was witnessing. He never once used the name Jesus, but his description of the rider on the white horse suggests to us that it is Jesus the Christ. He was described as "Faithful and True, righteous in all His dealings; His eyes were like blazing fire; on His head were many crowns . . . His title was The Word of God (Revelation 19:11, 13b). Jesus alone is worthy of such titles; He alone is the Word of God."

"The armies of heaven, dressed in the finest of pure white linen, followed Him on white horses. From His mouth came a sharp sword to strike down the nations. He will rule them with an iron rod. He will release the fierce wrath of God, the Almighty, like juice flowing from a winepress. On His robe at His thigh was written this title: King of all Kings and Lord of all Lords" (Revelation 19:14-16 NLT). All of the angelic hosts, the church-age saints including the martyrs, the Old Testament saints, and the tribulation saints will make up the armies of heaven. They will follow Christ to battle. They will be dressed in their righteous garments to be a part of this righteous war. But what glory! Christ, who is the Word of God, will be the Great Commander. The heavenly army that is accompanying Him will not have to fight. The sharp sword (Word of God) that proceeds from His mouth will strike down and defeat the nations. **"For it is my decision to gather together the kingdoms of the earth and pour out my fiercest anger and fury on them. All the earth will be devoured by the fire of my jealousy"** (Zephaniah 3:8b NLT).

The battle over evil was won by Jesus through His death and resurrection. This was the final consummation and all of heaven's armies will follow Christ to battle. But there was no fighting because the war had already been won. Jesus Christ, the King of all kings and the Lord over all lords, will be declared the Victor forever and ever! "We will walk through the valley in peace, with Jesus Himself as our Leader; we will walk through the valley in peace (Charles Albert Tindley), "We Shall Walk through the Valley."

"Then I saw an angel standing in the sun, shouting to the vultures flying high in the sky: Come, gather together for the great banquet

God has prepared. Come and eat the flesh of kings, generals, and strong warriors; of horses and their riders; and of all humanity, both free and slave, small and great. Then I saw the beast and the kings of this world and their armies gathered together to fight against the One sitting on the horse and His army" (Revelation 19:17-19 NLT). This great banquet prepared by God is known as the battle of Armageddon. This is the place where the last great battle between good and evil is fought. It will be a time when the flesh of all who refuse to register themselves for heaven by accepting the mark of the beast will be fed to the vultures.

"And the beast was captured, and with him the false prophet who did mighty miracles on behalf of the beast—miracles that deceived all who had accepted the mark of the beast and who worshipped his statue. Both the beast and his false prophet were thrown alive into the fiery lake of burning sulphur. Their entire army was killed by the sharp sword that came from the mouth of the One riding the white horse. And the vultures all gorged themselves on the dead bodies" (Revelation 19-20:21 NLT). The antichrist (the beast) and the false prophet will be captured alive and thrown into the lake of fire. They will not be killed by the sharp sword that came from the mouth of Jesus but will be thrown alive into the lake of fire—their final destiny. There they will await the arrival of Satan, his fallen angel, and all the souls who died outside Christ.

The flesh of kings, generals, strong warriors, horses and their riders, and of all humanity both great and small will be fed to vultures. All those who profaned the name of Jesus and worshipped the beast will be destroyed by the sharp sword that proceeds from the mouth of Jesus. "And God will provide rest for you who are being persecuted and also for us when the Lord Jesus appears from heaven. He will come with His mighty angels, in flaming fire, bringing judgment on those who don't know God and on those who refuse to obey the Good News of our Lord Jesus. They will be punished with eternal destruction, forever separated from the Lord and from His glorious power" (2 Thessalonians 1:7-9 NLT).

QUESTIONS FOR REVIEW

1. What was heaven's response to the punishment of the great prostitute and the avenging of the martyred saints?

2. Where does the word Hallelujah originate from and what does it mean in English?

3. What is one of the best kept secrets to overcoming evil?

4. Why were the saints in heaven rejoicing?

5. Who are the bride and guests of Christ?

6. Describe the apparel of the bride of Christ and what it represents.

7. Where and when will the marriage supper take place?

8. In a paragraph or two, describe the battle of Armageddon.

9. On what basis will we be rewarded at the believers' judgment?

10. Give a brief synopsis on the believers' crowns and where they may be found in Scriptures.

11. How do we as believers prepare ourselves to be the bride of Christ?

CHAPTER FIFTEEN

Thousand-Year Millennium Reign

Revelation 20

A Sin-Free World

"Then I saw an angel coming down from heaven with the key to the bottomless pit and a heavy chain in his hand. He seized the dragon—that old serpent, who is the devil, Satan—and bound him in chains for a thousand years. The angel threw him into the bottomless pit, which he then shut and locked so Satan could not deceive the nations anymore until the thousand years were finished. Afterward he must be released for a little while" (Revelation 20:1-3 NLT).

This world will be *sin-free* for a thousand years. The effects of sin will not be present on the earth. There will be no tempter to destroy or annoy. There will be no lack on the earth. There will be no evil on the earth to create lack. The power of evil was sealed in the bottomless pit.

During this period, the earth will have one King and His name is Jesus. "And the Lord will be King over all the earth. On that day there will be one Lord—His name alone will be worshipped" (Zechariah 14:9 NLT). He will reign over all the earth from sea to sea and shore to shore. Earth and heaven will be one in sweet harmony. "**The whole earth will** acknowledge the Lord and return to Him. People from every nation will bow down before Him. For the Lord is King! He rules all the nations" (Psalm 22:27 NLT). There will be complete peace on the earth. Everything concerning the saints will be perfected. This period of divine peace is known as the thousand-year millennium reign. Tim LaHaye wrote, "The binding of Satan will restrict him from doing the thing he does best, for the third verse says that he should deceive the nations no more till the thousand years shall be fulfilled. During the millennium Satan will not deceive men about themselves, God, Christ, or eternity. For this reason we conclude that the majority of people living then will be believers."[14]

It will be a world that is free of democracy, communism, capitalism, and all worldly governments. It will be heaven government ruling the earth for a thousand years. It will be a world without struggles, pain, poverty, sadness, sickness, disease, and disappointments. All of earth will experience the glory of rest that was disturbed by Satan in the garden of Eden. This earth will be covered with the glory of God. "For as the waters fill the sea, the earth will be filled with an awareness of the glory of the Lord" (Habakkuk 2:14 NLT). "And as the waters fill the sea, so the earth will be filled with people who know the Lord" (Isaiah 11:9b NLT).

This period known as the millennium reign was prophesied by Old Testament saints. "As my vision continued that night, I saw someone like a Son of Man coming with the clouds of heaven. He approached the Ancient One and was led into His Presence. He was given authority, honor, and sovereignty over all the nations of the world, so that people of every race and nation and language would obey Him" (Daniel 7:13-14a NLT). "And your King will bring peace to the nations. His realm will stretch from sea to sea and from the Euphrates River to the ends of the earth" (Zechariah 9:10b NLT). "Everyone will live in peace and prosperity, enjoying

---

14   Tim LaHaye, *Revelation Illustrated and Made Plain* (Grand Rapids Michigan: Zondervan Publishing, 1975), p. 278.

their own grapevines and fig trees, for there will be nothing to fear. The Lord of Heaven's Armies has made this promise!" (Micah 4:4 NLT). God spoke through them thousands of years before this set time that is being revealed to John. In Daniel's vision, the one who looked like "a Son of Man" is Jesus. Jesus used this passage out of Daniel several times in the gospel to refer to Himself. **"And in the future you will see me, the Son of Man, sitting at God's right hand in the place of power and coming back on the clouds of heaven"** (Matthew 26:64 NLT).

During this time, Satan will be chained and cast into the bottomless pit where he will be imprisoned for a thousand years. Who will God assign to cast Satan into the bottomless pit? Who is able to seize that old dragon, that ancient serpent, the Devil and bind him for a thousand years? Who but Jesus is able to cast him into the Abyss and lock and seal it over him? What is shut by Jesus can never be opened. He alone has the power and authority to break the lock and undo the seal. Even the devils themselves cannot break open what has been sealed by Jesus **"In this way, God disarmed the evil rulers and authorities. He shamed them publicly by His victory over them on the cross of Christ"** (Colossians 2:15 NLT).

The First Resurrection and the Second Death

"Then I saw thrones, and the people sitting on them had been given the authority to judge. And I saw the souls of those who had been beheaded for their testimony about Jesus and for proclaiming the word of God. They had not worshipped the beast or his statue, nor accepted his mark on their forehead or their hands. They all came to life again, and they reigned with Christ for a thousand years. This is the first resurrection. (The rest of the dead did not come back to life until the thousand years had ended.) Blessed and holy are those who share in the first resurrection. For them the second death holds no power, but they will be priests of God and of Christ and will reign with Him a thousand years" (Revelation 20:4-6 NLT).

Who was seated upon these thrones? They were the saints of all ages: The Old Testament saints, the New Testament saints, the tribulation saints, and the martyred saints, including the redeemed Jews. This is the first resurrection. Every child of God throughout the ages who suffers with Christ will reign with Him. "**If we endure hardship, we will reign with Him**" (2 Timothy 2:12 NLT). All those who die in Christ will be a part of the first resurrection, and they will reign with Him for a thousand years. This resurrection can also be called "The Glory Saints Resurrection." Only those who lived in and died for His glory will be a part of this first resurrection. The graves will be void of the bodies of God's people who were faithful to His cause, all the glorified saints of God. The souls of those who did not die in Christ will remain in their graves during the millennium reign.

The souls of the first resurrection will be sheltered from the second death—everlasting separation from God. They will be blessed and highly favored by God. They will be forever happy in the Lord. Tim LaHaye explains, "Man cannot enjoy uninterrupted blessing today because of sin. All those resurrected in the first or believer's resurrection will be resurrected holy. Thus the blessing of God, His original intent for man, will never be withheld, because man will live eternally holy and therefore eternally happy."[15] The first death is physical and will be experience by all (except the raptured saints). The second death is not physical but spiritual; those who die outside Christ will die to die again and will experience eternal separation from God. They will be a part of the sinner's judgment and will experience the eternal death sentence that will be pronounced upon Satan and all his followers. "**Indeed, the time is coming when all the dead in their graves will hear the voice of God's Son, and they will rise again. Those who have done good will rise to eternal life, and those who have continued in evil will rise to judgment**" (John 5:28b-29 NLT).

---

[15]   Tim LaHaye, *Revelation Illustrated and Made Plain* (Grand Rapids Michigan: Zondervan Publishing House, 1975), p. 282.

Ultimate Victory Over Evil

"When the thousand years end, Satan will be let out of his prison. He will go out to deceive the nations from every corner of the earth, which are called Gog and Magog. He will gather them for battle—a mighty host, as numberless as sand along the shore" (Revelation 20:7-8 NLT). When the millennium reign is ended, Satan will be released. His last rebellious act takes place in the eighth verse. It will be a futile final effort by Satan to try to come up against the army of God. He will try to deceive all the nations of the earth. Many will be deceived and they will gather with Satan and his army to fight against the people of God. Satan will seek revenge for his imprisonment.

"And I saw them as they went up the broad plain of the earth and surrounded God's people and the beloved city. But fire from heaven came down on the attacking armies and consumed them" (Revelation 20:9 NLT). The fire of God will destroy Satan and his army forever. God will always fight for His people. Always remember when the enemy is on the attack that God will have your back. He will set up an ambush that will always take your enemy down. This will be the ultimate victory over all the forces of evil. Satan's power is not eternal. He will meet his disastrous destiny.

"Then the devil, who betrayed them, was thrown into the lake of fire that burns with sulfur, joining the beast and the false prophet. There they will be tormented day and night forever and ever" (Revelation 20:10 NLT). This is the *ultimate* victory over evil. What glorious victory for the saints of God! All of heaven and earth waited for this time of ultimate deliverance out of the hand of Satan. The Devil is thrown into the lake of fire that burns with sulfur. He along with the antichrist and the false prophet will be tormented day and night forever and ever. There will never be another tempter to destroy or annoy the people of God. The earth will be finally free of evil not for a time but for all eternity . . . "It is finished the battle is over. It is finished there'll be no more war. It is finished the end of the conflict. It is finished and Jesus is Lord!" (Gloria and Bill Gaither, "It Is Finished"). **"For Christ must reign**

until He humbles all His enemies beneath His feet" (1 Corinthians 15:25 NLT).

Great White Throne Judgment

"And I saw a great white throne and the one sitting on it. The earth and sky fled from his presence, but they found no place to hide. I saw the dead, both great and small, standing before God's throne" (Revelation 20:11-12a NLT). The great white throne judgment is the final judgment for all sinners. This is the unbelievers' judgment. Every rebellious human being who rejects God's plan of salvation will be a part of this judgment. Unbelievers of all the ages will be a part of this judgment. People from all walks of life will be standing before the throne to be judged. The rich will be there and the poor. The morally good and the nice people will also be there. The kings and the queens, presidents, prime ministers, and other nobles will all be there.

Every soul that refuses to obey God will stand before the Great Judge on that day. Some church people will be there. Some Christian leaders will be there dressed in their self-righteous rags. There will be those who sang in the church choir or usher, even taught in Sunday schools, but never gave their lives to Christ—they will be a part of this sinners' judgment. There will be those who stood in the way of sinners while labeling themselves as believers. Can you begin to imagine the scene around the great white throne judgment?

"And the books were opened, including the Book of Life. And the dead were judged according to what they had done, as recorded in the books" (Revelation 20:12b NLT). The books will be opened including the Book of Life. What books is John referring too? The books that are opened are those that record the deeds of man. These books will tell the story of your earthly pilgrimage. Your life story will be revealed and everything that is now hidden will be made known. What will the books say concerning you and your earthly pilgrimage?

"The sea gave up the dead in it, and death and the grave were thrown into the lake of fire. This is the second death—the lake of fire. And anyone whose name was not found in the Book of Life was thrown into the lake of fire" (Revelation 20:13-15 NLT). The lake of fire is the final destination of all that is evil. The two last enemies to be destroyed are death and the grave. Death and the grave will be conquered and the legal rights to this earth will be fully in the hands of Jesus. The Lion of the tribe of Judah will prevail and He will reign forever and ever. Death and the grave will join Satan and his followers in the lake of fire and this will complete the judgment of God. They will no longer be a source of dread or fear. Their being will be forever extinct. All the souls that died outside Christ and were held by the sea will be released to judgment, and they were all thrown into the lake of fire. Are you ready for the books to be opened? Where will your soul spend eternity?

Tim LaHaye wrote, "Your name is already written in the Book of Life, but is it written in the Lamb's Book of Life? That depends entirely on what you have done with the Lord Jesus Christ. If you have accepted Him, it is; if you have not accepted Him, it is missing. The answer to the question determines your eternal destiny."[16] **"So stay awake and be prepared, because you do not know the day or hour of my return"** (Matthew 25:13 NLT).

---

[16] Tim LaHaye, *Revelation Illustrated and Made Plain* (Grand Rapids Michigan: Zondervan Publishing House, 1975), p. 305.

QUESTIONS FOR REVIEW

1. Describe the thousand-year millennium reign.

2. Where will Satan be during this time?

3. Describe the first resurrection.

4. Who will reign with Christ?

5. Where will the souls of those who did not die in Christ be during the millennium reign?

6. What is the second death?

7. Describe the ultimate victory over evil as presented in verse 10.

8. What is the great white throne judgment?

9. In verse 12, John is referring to what books?

10. Whose names will be written in the Lamb's Book of Life? Give reasons for your answer.

CHAPTER SIXTEEN

A New Age

Revelation 21

There is an old gospel song that says, "I'm tired of this world with its trouble and strife. I'm going to move someday." God has promised His overcoming church a new age, a better day. The kingdoms of this world will become the kingdoms of our God and of His Christ, and He shall reign forever and ever! It's a timeless glory reign! One day this old age with all its trouble and strife, all of its maladies and inadequacies, will be no more. This world is quickly passing away and we will be moving into a new age someday.

"God has set (planted) eternity in the hearts of men" (Ecclesiastes 3:11b NLT). The body that houses us is temporal, terrestrial; it has an expiration date, but our souls are eternal and one day this body will expire and we will come up out of this shell. Our eternal soul will make its way to either heaven or hell. Man can never be satisfied by temporal gain. There is a great void yearning that no earthly substance is able to satisfy. Only that which is eternal can satisfy the heart of man and fill the void in his life. No matter how great his earthly accomplishments are, he will still not be satisfied. There will always be that void, that emptiness. The more you get from this world, the more you want and the more you go after. Earthly gain can never satisfy the deep longing of man's soul.

True contentment lies beyond the realm of earth because of what has been planted in man's heart by His Creator. Temporal things and gains can never satisfy the soul. Eternity has been planted in our hearts; we are eternity beings, and there will always be that void that nothing but Jesus can fill. Our desire for a perfect world can only be found in God's new age.

"Then I saw a new heaven and a new earth, for the old heaven and the old earth had disappeared. And the sea was gone" (Revelation 21:1). This world in which we live will one day disappear along with the sea. It will all pass away. It will all be destroyed one day. The very foundation of this earth (as we know it) has been laid on the seas and God established it upon the depth of the ocean. He is the owner and Creator of this world. **"The earth is the Lord's, and the fullness thereof; the world, and they that dwell therein. For He had founded it upon the seas, and established it upon the floods"** (Psalm 24:1-2 KJV). The manifestation of this new age will require the complete annihilation of this present heaven and earth. This vast universe—stars, galaxies, and all elements— will all be destroyed. During Noah's time, the earth was destroyed by water, but on the day of judgment it will be destroyed by fire. **"And God has also commanded that the heavens and the earth will be consumed by fire on the Day of Judgment, when ungodly people will perish"** (2 Peter 3:7 NLT). All traces of evil will be erased as though it never existed. The new heaven and earth will be the final home of God and the faithful redeemed. It will be a place void of imperfection. It will be a gloryland where the faithful believers will spend eternity.

The human mind is unable to conceive or fathom what this new heaven and earth will be like. It will be completely different from this present heaven and earth. There will be no more sea. We cannot envision an earth without sea. The psalmist said that it was founded (laid) upon the seas and built on the ocean depths. It is said that two-thirds of this present earth's surface is covered with water. One-third includes mountains and deserts void of habitation, and just a small portion is inhabited. But on that great day, every mountain, desert, valley, sea, heaven, and indeed all of earth will all disappear. **"For this world is not** our home; we are looking forward to our city in heaven, which is yet to come" (Hebrews 13:14 NLT).

"And I saw the holy city, the new Jerusalem, coming down from God out of heaven like a beautiful bride prepared for her husband" (Revelation 21:2 NLT). John saw the holy city, the New Jerusalem, coming down from heaven. This New Jerusalem is not something God is piecing together at present but was designed by God before the very foundation of the world. It's being kept in heaven for God's set time. This city that is in heaven will make its descent ushering in the age of completion and perfection. It's a city that has been prepared for God's bride whose names are written in the Lamb's Book of Life. The bride will be taken into the Bridegroom chamber for consummation of this eternal marriage, and forever to be with Him. The writer of Hebrews describes this city as a continuing (never-ending) city whose architect is God. **"Abraham did this because he was confidently looking forward to a city with eternal foundations, a city designed and built by God"** (Hebrews 11:10 NLT). Abraham and the other prophets of old waited and longed for this city to come.

In this New Jerusalem, God will make His abode with man. There will be no political government to rule this new age. It will be the throne of God, a spiritual government with God Himself as our leader. "I **heard a loud shout from the throne saying, 'Look, the home of God is now among His people! He will live with them, and they will be His people. God Himself will be with them'"** (Revelation 21:3 NLT). God's throne will no longer be in the third heaven but in the New Jerusalem. We will enjoy uninterrupted fellowship, communion with God. Our faith will be turned to sight. We will see Him as He is. The season for struggling with our faith will be over. Our faith will be made sight. We will behold Him as He is in all His splendor, majesty, holiness, and righteousness. We will live with Him and He with us forever. No longer will we have to pray the heavens open for God's glory to be revealed, but we the redeemed of the Lord will be living in the glory forever and ever! Like the New Jerusalem, we will be covered in God's glory. What a time it will be! Our souls will look back and wonder how we got over.

"And God shall wipe away all tears from their eyes and there shall be no more death, neither sorrow nor crying, neither shall there be any more pain: for the former things are passed away" (Revelation 21:4 KJV). As a believer in the new age world order, you will never cry again. God Himself, the tender, loving, compassionate Father, will wipe away all tears. God, not an angel, will wipe away all tears. There will be one wipe of the eyes and there will be no more tears for all eternity. How great is our God!

The great white throne judgment will be the last time a faithful believer cries. We will cry for the souls that we did not take the time to minister to; we will cry for the many missed opportunities of prayer and being God's hand extended. We will cry for our loved ones, friends, neighbors, pastors, bishops, and all those standing outside the portals of glory. We will cry for them when we hear the words "Depart from me . . ." But the loving, tender, compassionate God will wipe away the believers' tears forever.

The tears in this passage may also represent all human sorrow, tragedy, failure, pain, and disappointment. We will never shed these types of tears again. There will be no disappointment in heaven. There will be no pain, sorrow, tragedy, failure, or affliction. What a beautiful place heaven must be! Even the memory of yesterdays will be erased by God. The saints will say, "Good bye," to the former maladies of life. The memory of that which *used* to make you cry—every heartache, pain, and rejection—will be erased. What an awesome God! The saints will cry no more. It will finally be over. The Bible says, **"For the old world and its evil are gone forever"** (Revelation 21:4b NLT).

The causes of trouble, trials, sorrows, sickness, affliction, heartache, and disappointments will all be gone forever. The causes will be destroyed. The former things will pass away! We will experience perfect peace and rest in this new age. It will be totally free from the very tinge of evil.

He will make all things new for the saints' pleasure to be enjoyed for all eternity. The full measure of Him being the God of all comfort will be experienced by the inhabitants of this new age. It will be an eternal reign of glory.

"And He also said, 'It is finished! I am the Alpha and the Omega—the Beginning and the End. To all who are thirsty I will give the springs of the water of life without charge'" (Revelation 21:6 NLT). God identifies Himself as Alpha and Omega. He wipes away the memory of your horrid past from the beginning to the end! When God wipes away the tears of the believers, He will be wiping as Alpha and Omega, everything from the beginning of your life to the very end. It will be finished; the battles of live will be over. There will be no battle to fight in that new age. As the redeemed, we will be the inheritors of eternal life and everything; every blessing within that new age will be ours and we will drink from the springs of the water of life free of charge. Jim Hill wrote, "All is peace forevermore, on that happy golden shore. What a day, glorious day that will be!" ("What a Day That Will Be," 1955.) No more hospitals, prisons, institutions, whorehouses, or drughouses; it will all be over! A timeless age is coming that will be totally free from the very trace of imperfection or evil! Everything (including you and I) will be made new!

"He that overcometh shall inherit all things; and I will be his God, and he shall be my son. But the fearful, and unbelieving, the abominable, and murderers and whoremongers, and sorcerers, and idolaters, and all liars, shall have their part in the lake of fire and brimstone which is the second death" (Revelation 21:7-8 KJV). God Himself declares who will inherit the blessings of the new age. The inheritors of the blessings will be those who overcome, the faithful ones, those who kept the faith in spite of the pressure. Those who endured and kept on praising, kept on praying, kept on serving, kept on worshipping, kept on seeking. **"He who is victorious (overcomes) will inherit all this!"** We have the treasure in these earthen vessels to overcome every hour of temptation and trial. Keep on overcoming; payday is coming after awhile. There is a great reward for the overcoming saints. They are the victorious ones who will inherit the full measure of the Father's blessings. Those who do not overcome will not be a part of the blessings of this new age. On that day, they will be sentenced to a Christless hell.

It doesn't matter how you shout and praise in the worship service. Unless you exercise faith and become an overcomer, you will not be a part of this glory city. If you succumb (let the weight of this hour overpower you), you will not overcome. Have a made up mind that you are going all the way with God. Overcome that situation; overcome that temptation. Don't allow the enemy to distract you, shake your faith, and frustrate you. Overcome! You have faith to go the distance . . . Keep moving! Don't give up; suicide is not an option. Overcome continual depression and frustration. Overcome! You have the victory in Jesus' name! As believers, we are on the winning team! Don't mind what you may be going through or what people may say about you. All of your struggles will soon be over! You have a reserved place in that New Jerusalem. It was paid for by the blood of the Lamb and it's all yours.

It was never God's original plan for man to be a part of hell's fire. But all who turn away from God—the cowards (those who valued man's opinion more than God's), the unbelievers, the corrupted, the murderers, the immoral, those who practice witchcraft, idol worshippers, and all liars—will experience the "second death," which is the lake of fire. They will join Satan, the antichrist, the false prophet, death, the grave, and the fallen angels in the lake that burns with fire and sulfur. They will enter into eternal torment and separation from God. The hour of repentance will be over and there will be no way for man to reconcile with God.

"Then one of the seven angels who held the seven bowls containing the seven last plagues came and said to me, 'Come with me! I will show you the bride, the wife of the Lamb. So he took me in spirit to a great, high mountain, and he showed me the holy city, Jerusalem, descending out of heaven from God. It was filled with the glory of God and sparkled like a precious gem, crystal clear like jasper'" (Revelation 21:9-11 NLT). John is taken in the Spirit to a great high mountain and is shown the bride, the Lamb's wife. The city itself is not the bride, but the inhabitants of the city, the overcoming, victorious ecclesia, are the bride. The ecclesia that has gone from glory to glory proclaiming the gospel story will be the glorious bride of Christ. The holy city, Jerusalem, will be inhabited with the triumphant saints of all the ages.

Every overcoming saint will be in that city. Abraham and Sarah will be there. Moses, David, Elijah, and Elisha will all be there. Jeremiah and Isaiah will be there. Peter, Paul, and all the rapture and tribulation saints will be there. And yes, I will be there! Will you be there? It will be a people-filled glory city that is coming down. There is a city that has been prepared for the saints, the bride of Christ in heaven. Some call it paradise; some call it the gloryland. It doesn't matter what it is called. It is good to know that whether we die or are raptured, we will be a part of that city that is coming down.

It will be no ordinary plane ride, no ordinary plane landing, as this city makes its way down out of heaven and into earth's realm. No one will be on the runway taxiing in this city and telling it where to park. But God Himself will rule supreme. And this will be a new heaven and a new earth making a descent out of God's heaven, and it will happen suddenly. It will come down in God's time and at heaven's speed. It will be a twinkling-of-the-eye experience for the overcoming believers who will be the inhabitants of this city. John said the city shone with the glory of God. It's a city filled with glory; it's a glory city. The glory of God will cause this city to sparkle like precious gems. He will establish His throne in this New Jerusalem. He Himself will be our leader forever and ever. The old folks used to sing, "I've a home prepared where the saints abide . . . just over in the gloryland." This city is truly the gloryland. It's a square city surrounded with a ball of crystal light reflecting the glory of God, because all of God's glory is in the city. "**It shone with the glory of God and sparkled like a precious stone-like jasper as clear as crystal**" (Revelation 21:11 NLT). "**When he measured it, he found it was a square, as wide as it was long**" (Revelation 21:16a NLT).

"Its walls were broad and high, with twelve gates guarded by twelve angels. And the names of the twelve tribes of Israel were written on the gates. There were three gates on each side—east, north, south, and west. The wall of the city had twelve foundation stones, and on them were written the names of the twelve apostles of the Lamb" (Revelation 21:12-14 NLT). John tries to describe the makeup of this city. The walls suggest the security of those within the new world order. It will serve as a constant reminder that all the inhabitants of this new age will be forever secured in the presence of the Lord. What a comforting thought; we will never again be separated from the presence of the Lord. "And so shall we ever be with the Lord. Wherefore comfort one another with these words" (1 Thessalonians 4:17b-18 KJV).

John saw great high walls and twelve gates that were all guarded by angels and the names of the twelve tribes of Israel were written on the gates. The names of the twelve apostles of Jesus are written on the twelve foundation stones. John Eldon Ladd, in his book *A Commentary on the Revelation of John*, wrote, "This is an obvious allusion to the theology of the church, which is built upon the foundation of the apostles and prophets (Ephesians 2:20). By this symbolism of the twelve gates bearing the names of the twelve tribes of Israel, and the twelve foundations bearing the names of the twelve apostles, John indicates that the city encompasses both dispensations and that both the Israel of the Old Testament and of the church of the New Testament have their place in God's final establishment."[17] The city will be made up of believing Jews and Gentiles, those who have been faithful to God throughout the Old Testament and the New Testament era. We will all be the inhabitants of this glory city, and Jesus who became our Gate will usher us into this city.

"The angel who talked to me held in his hand a gold measuring stick to measure the city, its gates, and its wall. When he measured it, he found it was a square, as wide as it was long. In fact, it was in the form

---

[17]   George Eldon Ladd, *A Commentary on the Revelation of John* (Grand Rapids Michigan: Wm. B. Eerdmans Publishing Co., 1987), p. 281.

of a cube, for its length and width and height were each 1,400 miles. Then he measured the walls and found them to be 216 feet thick (the angel used a standard human measure)" (Revelation 21:15-17 NLT). The numbers of this New Jerusalem suggest to us the perfection of the city. It will be a perfect city whose builder and ruler is God.

It will be a void of imperfection and in verses 18-21, John continues to try to describe this glory city. "The wall was made of Jasper, and the city was pure gold, as clear as glass. The wall of the city was built on foundation stones inlaid with twelve gems; the first was jasper, the second sapphire, the third agate, the fourth emerald, the fifth onyx, the sixth carnelian, the seventh chrysolite, the eight beryl, the ninth topaz, the tenth chrysoprase, the eleventh jacinth, the twelfth amethyst. The twelve gates were made of pearls—each gate from a single pearl! And the main street was pure gold, as clear as glass" (Revelation 21:18-21 NLT).

It is a city and its measurements are approximately 1,400 miles. It is as wide as it is long. The city walls are 144 cubits (216 feet) thick (by man's measurement). The walls are made of jasper and the city is pure gold. The foundation of the city is decorated with precious stones. The twelve gates are twelve pearls and each gate made of a single pearl. The streets are pure gold as transparent as glass. It is the same shape as the Most Holy Place in Solomon's temple. "Solomon prepared the inner sanctuary in the rear of the Temple, where the Ark of the Lord's covenant would be placed. This inner sanctuary was 30 feet long, 30 feet wide and 30 feet high. Solomon overlaid its walls and ceiling with pure gold. He also overlaid the altar made of cedar" (1 Kings 6:20 NLT).

"No Temple could be seen in the city, for the Lord God Almighty and the Lamb are its Temple. And the city has no need of the sun, for the glory of God illuminates the city, and the Lamb is its light" (Revelation 21:22-23 NLT). There is no need for a temple in the new age; the shekinah presence of God is everywhere. It will cover the city. You will not be able to get away from the presence of God. But continued fellowship will be experienced by all of the inhabitants for all eternity.

There is no need for the sun or moon in this New Jerusalem. In this new age, you will never experience darkness again. The presence, the glory of God, and the Lamb will be its light.

"The nations of the earth will walk in its light, and the rulers of the world will come and bring their glory to it. Its gates never close at the end of day because there is no night" (Revelation 21:24-25 NLT). The presence of God will banish all darkness and night from the city. You will never experience tiredness in this city. There will be continual rest. The presence of God will flood the city. The brightness of His glory will be its only light. The city gates will never close. Jesus has become our gate, and even in eternity He will never cease to be our gate.

"Nothing evil will be allowed to enter—no one who practices shameful idolatry and dishonesty—but only those whose names are written in the Lamb's Book of Life" (Revelation 21:27 NLT). It is a new age that has been prepared for the Overcoming ecclesia. Only those whose names are written in the Lamb's Book of Life will be in this new age-New World Order. We all need to secure our citizenship in this New Jerusalem. Authentic Christians, genuine Christians will be a part of this new age. Those who not only name the name of Jesus but those who live for Jesus names will be in the Lamb's Book of Life. The matters of your heart will determine whether your Christianity (your faith) is real. Your being morally correct will not qualify you for this new age. Hell will have a lot of morally good folks in it. Your singing in the choir or ushering will not qualify you. There will be many Christian singers, ushers, Sunday school teachers and preachers in hell. It's the truth in the inner parts that will seal your final destiny. **"Behold, thou desirest truth in the inward parts"** (Psalm 51:6 NLT). **God blesses those whose hearts are pure, for they will see God"** (Matthew 5:8 NLT).

"But when the Son of Man comes in His glory, and all the angels with Him, then He will sit upon His glorious throne. All the nations will be gathered in His Presence, and He will separate them as a Shepherd separates the sheep from the goats. He will place the sheep at His right hand and the goats at His left. Then the King will

say to those on the right, 'Come, you who are blessed by my Father, inherit the Kingdom prepared for you from the foundation of the world'" (Matthew 25:31-34 NLT). There are far more souls on their way to heaven than there are who are on their way to hell. Satan is not the winner. Jesus is! Make your calling and election a sure thing so that you too will hear Him say, "Come, you who are blessed by My Father, inherit the kingdom prepared for you from the foundation of the world." Charles H. Gabriel wrote, "Oh, that will be glory for me, glory for me, glory for me. When by His grace I shall look on His face, that will be glory, be glory for me" ("Oh, That Will Be Glory").

This world has an expiration date stamped on it. It will not last forever. There is going to be a new age and a new world order where God and God alone will rule from eternity to eternity. There will be no devil to annoy. The tempter's reign will be over for all eternity. So hold on and go through what you been going through, keep pressing, keep loving, keep serving, keep giving, keep praying, keep thanking, keep praising, keep worshipping, keep seeking. The best is yet to come. When your soul is resting in the presence of the Lord, only then will you be satisfied!

QUESTIONS FOR REVIEW

1. Who will be a part of this new age, and what are the blessings they will inherit?

2. Why will there be no need for the sun and the moon in this new age?

3. Describe the New Jerusalem.

4. Who will be the inhabitants of this new city?

5. Who is the bride of Christ?

6. Who will experience the second death, the lake of fire?

7. In this chapter, what do tears represent?

8. How does one secure one's citizenship in this new age?

CONCLUSION

Life Forever in the Glory

Revelation 22

The book of Revelation is all about the reign of glory. Even as it was in the beginning, so shall it be in the end. This world will be covered by the glory of God. We are about to experience accelerated glory as the plans of God unfold on the earth. Jesus will reign forever and ever, and of His kingdom there will be no end.

In the beginning, the whole world was the kingdom of God. God reigned from east to west, north to south. All of the earth was God's domain covered with the knowledge of His glory. God's reign covered the earth as the waters covered the sea. Man and all creation were crowned with the glory of God. "**For you made us only a little lower than God, and you crowned us with glory and honor**" (Psalm 8:5 NLT). He lived in the righteousness of God. Everything was created with everlasting power. This earth was filled with the life of God. There was no fading away or death on the earth. God's reign was sovereign; His presence, power, and glory were everywhere.

God placed man in the garden and gave him authority to rule the earth. He gave man dominion, power, and control over all the earth. There was no fear or weakness in man. Man was perfect in all his ways. Man did not have to worry about being attacked by wild animals or becoming depleted in anyway. The glory of God had him covered. His every need was supplied by God. In Genesis 2, God provided a companion to help the man. Man's life was complete in God.

But when man decided to doubt God's goodness and listen to the serpent, he fell from glory, that perfect state of being. The earth was now opened to evil and man was no longer covered with the glory of God. He found himself naked, void of covering. Even today man is the only one of God's animals that is naked and in need of clothing. What a costly fall! Man fell from grace and gave the controls of earth to Satan. Satan became the god of this world. "**Satan, the god of this evil world, has blinded the minds of those who don't believe, so they are unable to see the glorious light of the Good News that is shining upon them**" (2 Corinthians 4:4a NLT).

God could not leave man in his fallen position. Man was His precious creation in His image and likeness. He sent Jesus to bridge the gap between Him and man. Jesus was sent to redeem, to restore man back to God. Through His blood, the great transaction was made. And now man no longer has to stay in that fallen condition but can be reconciled to God. "**He took His own blood, and with it secured our salvation forever**" (Hebrews 9:12b NLT).

In this final chapter, we see where man will once again experience the fullness of God's glory. It will be a new beginning for man. The saints of every age will be a part of this new beginning. It will not be just a new season, but this will be eternal; forever we will be abiding in the New Jerusalem. It will be the perfect ending to this life story. In the New Jerusalem, the blessings are continuous, eternal, never ending. We, the overcoming saints, will enter into our eternal Sabbath rest. Free from every form of darkness.

"**And the angel showed me a pure river with the water of life, clear as crystal, flowing from the throne of God and of the Lamb, coursing down the center of the main street. On each side of the river grew** a Tree of Life, bearing twelve crops of fruit, with a fresh crop each month. The leaves were used for medicine to heal the nations" (Revelation 22:1-2 NLT). In chapter 21, John told us about the descent of the New Jerusalem and gave us a vivid description of the city where we will live for all eternity. Now in this chapter he shares with us "The Delights of the New Jerusalem." It's a glory city that is free from every form of evil, a place of splendor covered with the intricate beauty and splendor of God' presence.

One of the first things John was shown was the river of life that flows from the throne of God. This glory city is invincible; it is eternal. The life-giving energy of God will sustain eternal life in the holy city. The eternal life in the city will be sustained by the reign of God and the Lamb. All life in the city will flow from the throne of God and the Lamb. Old Testament writings support the fact that there is a river that is flowing from the throne of God. The Psalmist wrote, "**There is a river, the streams whereof shall make glad the city of God, the holy place of the tabernacles of the Most High. God is in the midst of her; she shall not be moved**" (Psalm 46:4-5a KJV).

There is no life outside God, and the closer one gets to God through Jesus, the more alive one becomes. The connection to God can only be made through Jesus, the Lamb. Jesus said, "**If any man thirst let him come unto me, and drink. He that believeth on me, as the Scripture hath said, out of his belly shall flow rivers of living water**" (John 7:37-38 KJV). It is only those who heed the call of Jesus to drink now who will be the inhabitants of the glory city. They will be the redeemed, blood-washed saints that will experience eternal glory blessings.

In John's vision, the Tree of Life was situated on either side of the river of life. There was not just a river of life but a Tree of Life. This tree was watered by the river of life that flows from the throne of God. The fruitfulness of the tree and the leaves being used for medicine symbolizes that there will be no barrenness and nothing to cause sickness or harm in the New Jerusalem. The glory of God will be our eternal shade. The vitality, vigor, strength, and life of God will sustain life within the city.

We will experience true joy, peace, and contentment in the everlasting presence of God. Matthew Henry wrote, "The presence of God in heaven is the health and happiness of the saints. There they find in Him a remedy for all their former maladies (moral and mental disorder) and are preserved by Him in the most healthful and vigorous state."[18]

"No longer will anything be cursed. For the throne of God and of the Lamb will be there, and His servants will worship Him" (Revelation 22:3 NLT). There will be total freedom and eternal life forever in God's holy city. The roses will never fade. The trees will never need to be pruned or the grass mowed. Everything including the agriculture will be perfect in the New Jerusalem. The curse that was brought about because of the fall of man will not be present in this New Jerusalem. The curse is over and the earth will never be cursed again. The city will be free from all evil, curses, mishaps, and temptations. The saints will never again be disturbed by Satan. He will never be able again to lure us away from the presence of God. His destruction will be final. We will forever enjoy the delights of the New Jerusalem. **"And Jerusalem will be filled, safe at last, never again to be cursed and destroyed"** (Zechariah 14:11 NLT).

"And they will see His face, and His name will be written on their foreheads" (Revelation 22:4 NLT). Imagine the joy of the saints when our faith is made sight! There will be inexpressible joy when we are able to gaze into the face of God and the Lamb. It will not be just a quick glimpse of His face, but forever we will behold Him face-to-face. This will be the greatest happiness of the saints—to dwell in the presence of the Lord forever. In Psalm 17, David wrote, **"But because I have done what is right, I will see you. When I awake, I will be fully satisfied, for I will see you face to face"** (Psalm 17:15 NLT). The ultimate goal of every believer is to see God face to face and to experience full rest in His eternal presence.

---

18   Matthew Henry, *Matthew Henry Commentary, Volume 6* (United States of America: Hendrickson Publishing, Inc., 1991), p. 954.

In our mortal bodies, we are still capable of making wrong decisions and yielding to the work of the flesh. But in the New Jerusalem, we will be clothed in our immortal bodies and God will have complete ownership of His saints. We will not be tempted to sin. The reign of the tempter will be over. It will be all glory in that holy city. We will forever walk in the light of the presence of God and the Lamb. "**And there will be no night there—no need for lamps or sun—for the Lord God will shine on them. And they will reign forever and ever**" (Revelation 22:5 NLT).

"**Look, I am coming soon! Blessed are those who obey the prophecy written in this scroll**" (Revelation 22:7 NLT). Three times in this chapter Jesus told John that His return was soon. In verse 12, He said, "**See, I am coming soon, and my reward is with me, to repay all according to their deeds.**" And again in verse 20. "**He who is the faithful witness to all these things says, "Yes, I am coming soon!"**" We are encouraged to keep looking for His imminent return. And those who remain faithful and are obedient to the prophetic voice throughout the book of Revelation will be blessed. Will you be one of them?

Jesus' coming could take place at any moment. And when He comes, His reward is with Him to give to the faithful believers their just recompense. And as though to further encourage the faithful believers, in verse 20 He reiterates this glorious truth. "**Yes, I am coming soon!**" The Amplified Bible says, "**Surely, I am coming quickly, speedily, swiftly.**" How ready are you for His soon return? Are you in pursuit of His glory? What have you done recently for Christ that will last, that will stand the test upon His return?

"**Blessed are those who wash their robes so they can enter through the gates of the city and eat the fruit from the Tree of Life. Outside the city are the dogs—the sorcerers, the sexually immoral, the murderers, the idol worshipers, and all who love to live a lie**" (Revelation 22:14-15 NLT). The washing of the robes symbolizes those who are washed in the blood of the Lamb. The righteous, victorious saints will eat from the Tree of Life, will experience the delights of the New Jerusalem. Paul warned the church in Rome to be ready for the "at any moment" return of Jesus. "The night is nearly over; the day is almost here. So let us put aside the deeds of darkness and put on the armor of light. Let us behave decently, as in the daytime, not in orgies and drunkenness, not in sexual immorality and debauchery, not in dissension and jealousy. Rather clothe yourselves with the Lord Jesus Christ, and do not think about how to gratify the desires of the sinful nature" (Romans 13:12-14 KJV).

"The Spirit and the bride say, 'Come.' Let each one who hears them say, 'Come.' Let the thirsty come—anyone who wants to. Let them come and drink the water of life without charge" (Revelation 22:17 NLT). Today the Holy Spirit and the bride (the ecclesia) are saying, "Come to Jesus." The cry is for all people from all nations to come and accept God's plan of salvation. It is not God's will that any should perish. The Bible says, "Today you must listen to His voice. Don't harden your hearts against Him as Israel did when they rebelled" (Hebrews 3:15 NLT). May all who read this book hearken to the cry of the Holy Spirit and the bride and come to Jesus.

"And I solemnly declare to everyone who hears the prophetic words of this book: If anyone adds to what is written here, God will add to that person the plagues described in this book. And if anyone removes any of the words of this prophetic book, God will remove that person's share in the Tree of Life and in the holy city that are described in this book" (Revelation 22:18-19 NLT). This is a strong warning not to be careless with what is written in this book. We must take it seriously and not add or take away from the prophecies. As believers, let us hold fast to the great truth of these prophecies without trying to alter what has been given. We should not try to add human interpretation or explanation to these written prophecies. To do so will mean eternal separation from God.

"He who is the faithful witness to all these things says, 'Yes, I am coming soon!' Amen! Come, Lord Jesus! The grace of the Lord Jesus be with you all" (Revelation 22:20-21 NLT). The book of Revelation ends with a beseeching plea. **"Come, Lord Jesus!"** After experiencing the glory of revelation, John's cry was, "Come, Lord Jesus!" The Revelator recognized that this world with all its evil will quickly come to an end. There is hope for all who listen and take heed to the words that are written in this book. In a world where wrong seems right and right seems wrong, the believers are encouraged to keep faith alive and press on. An eternal paradise is waiting for you with *all* the delights of glory.

<u>Finish the Race</u>

"For God had far better things in mind for us that would also benefit them for they can't receive the prize at the end of the race until we finish the race" (Hebrews 11:40 NLT). Quite often we forget that we are only *sojourners*, temporary residents of this earth. Not one of us is here to stay. We are all in a race—the race of life—and how well we run will determine our permanent place of abode at the end of the day. Paul knew that the final chapter of his life was about to end. He knew that he was nearing the finishing line. He was confident that he had run a good race and that his life was poured out as a drink offering for the sake of the gospel.

Paul persevered and never gave up. Yes, he had his off days, but he kept on running. He was determined to finish the race. You must be determined like Paul to finish the race. Every day you must have a made-up mind to journey on. You ran through some stuff yesterday and may have to run through some today, but don't look back; finish the race. You must not give up; keep on running. The battle is never greater than your God who controls the day. Paul was never deterred. He remained focused and kept running even when he was imprisoned. You must run even when you feel imprisoned. Keep your eyes fixed on the goal and the Finisher of life, Jesus Christ.

At the end of our race, let us all be able to say like Paul. **"As for me, my life has already been poured out as an offering to God. The time of my death is near. I have fought a good fight. I have finished the race, and I have remained faithful. And now the prize awaits me—the**

**crown of righteousness that the Lord, the righteous Judge, will give
on that great day of His return. And the prize is not just for me but
for all who eagerly look forward to His glorious return"** (2 Timothy
4:6-8 NLT).

The faith runners—Old Testament and New Testament saints in
heaven—are waiting for us to finish the race. In the book of Hebrews,
we are told that we have a great crowd of witnesses cheering us on
to the finish line. There is harmony among Old Testament and New
Testament believers. We will all be glorified together, and what a day
that will be! Their overcoming testimonies encourage us to run on,
despite the pressures of life, and to finish the race.

Jesus' return is imminent. It is not something that we the believers in
Christ are hoping will happen. But it will happen, just like he said, in the
twinkling of an eye. He will not come again as Mary's boy child born in a
manger. But He will come as the glorious King to take His bride out of
this sin-sick world. He will take us to our new eternal glory home where
He will reign as King of Kings and Lord of Lords forever and ever, world
without end. Amen! *The glory of Revelation!*

QUESTIONS FOR REVIEW

1. In the book of Genesis, what happened when man fell from glory?

2. How is man redeemed back to God?

3. What will sustain eternal life in the New Jerusalem?

4. What does the fruitfulness of the tree and the leaves being used as medicine symbolize?

5. Describe the freedom in the New Jerusalem.

6. What should be the ultimate goal of every believer?

7. In verse 14, what does the washing of the robe symbolize?

8. What have you done recently for Christ that will last, that will stand the test upon His return?

9. After experiencing the glory of revelation, what was John's cry?

10. After reading this book, what is your cry and why?

References

Ladd, Eldon George. *A Commentary on the Revelation of John*, Grand Rapids, Michigan: Williams B. Eerdmans Publishing Company, 1972.

LaHaye, Timothy. *Revelation Illustrated and Made Plain*, Grand Rapids, Michigan: Zondervan Publishing House, 1975.

Wiersbe, Warren W. *The Bible Exposition Commentary, Volume II*, Colorado Springs: David C. Cook, 1989.

Henry, Matthew. *Matthew Henry's Commentary on the Whole Bible*, United States of America: Hendrickson Publishers, Inc., 1991.

Dake, Jennings Finis, Reverend. *God's Plan for Man*, Lawrenceville, Georgia: Dake Bible Sales, Inc., 1983.

Pfeiffer, Charles F. *The New Combined Bible Dictionary and Concordance*, Grand Rapids, Michigan: Baker Book House, 1961.

MacArthur, John Jr. *The MacArthur New Testament Commentary, Revelation 1-11*, Chicago, Illinois: Moody Publishers, 1999.

Wallace, Susan J. *Revelation Simplified*, Freeport, Grand Bahamas: Access Publishing, 2005.

Zondervan's Compact Bible Dictionary, Grand Rapids, Michigan, 1993.

Life Application Study Bible NLT, Wheaton, Illinois: Tyndale House Publishers, Inc., 1988.

Life in the Spirit Study Bible NIV, Grand Rapids, Michigan: Zondervan Publishing House, 1973.

Holy Bible, People's Parallel Edition KJV, Wheaton, Illinois: Tyndale House Publishers, Inc., 1997.

The New Strong's Complete Dictionary of Bible Words, Nashville, Tennessee: Thomas Nelson Publishers, 1996.